More Praise fo...
GRIEF

"One of the strengths of Cholbi's book is in the range of authors from whom he takes accounts of grief: from the personal disclosures of C. S. Lewis to Joan Didion to the fiction of Tolstoy, Camus, and Shakespeare, just to name a few. . . . Excellent. . . . *Grief* certainly fulfills its aim of encouraging other philosophers to consider the existential phenomenon of grief. Cholbi has prompted such a conversation here in a significant, thoroughgoing, and engaging way."
—BRAD DEFORD, *Philosophy in Review*

"There is much to like about Cholbi's book. It is short, densely argued, and shows great familiarity with the relevant philosophical, literary, and psychological literatures."
—JOHN DANAHER, *Philosopher's Magazine*

"A clever, deeply touching book, *Grief* adds to the growing canon of important, thoughtful writing on this inevitable stage of life that we all need to understand and learn more about. Taking a new, philosophical perspective, Michael Cholbi invites us to think in a way that is accessible but serious—we are all philosophers after all."
—JULIET ROSENFELD, author of *The State of Disbelief: A Story of Death, Love, and Forgetting*

"Socrates claimed that all of philosophy is training for death, but philosophers have nevertheless been strangely silent on bereavement and grief. Fortunately, we now have Michael Cholbi's book, which takes us through the key philosophical questions about grief. Revolving around the paradox of grief—that it is painful yet valuable—Cholbi writes clearly and wisely about this fundamental human phenomenon. I recommend this book to anyone who is interested in grief: philosophers, humanists, and general readers will all benefit from it."
—SVEND BRINKMANN, author of *Grief: The Price of Love*

"Informed, erudite, and humane, this outstanding book investigates the scope, nature, value, and rationality of grief, presenting a 'qualified optimism' against accounts that see grief as a weakness, a source of shame, and a threat to our humanity. Cholbi skillfully deploys resources from philosophy, psychology, psychiatry, literature, and medicine to enhance our understanding of grief, and the book will be of great interest to all those working in these fields, and indeed any of us who want to know more about this central but philosophically neglected element of human experience."
—MICHAEL S. BRADY, author of *Suffering and Virtue*

"An engaging and illuminating contribution to the philosophy of death, *Grief* advances a novel and surprising account of what grief is and what makes it rationally defensible, valuable, and perhaps even obligatory. A humane, thoughtful, and insightful book, *Grief* will be invaluable to sociologists, anthropologists, psychologists, and psychiatrists, while general readers will also find it accessible and compelling."
—PATRICK STOKES, author of *Digital Souls: A Philosophy of Online Death*

Grief

Grief

A PHILOSOPHICAL GUIDE

Michael Cholbi

PRINCETON UNIVERSITY PRESS

PRINCETON AND OXFORD

Published by Princeton University Press
41 William Street, Princeton, New Jersey 08540
99 Banbury Road, Oxford OX2 6JX

press.princeton.edu

Library of Congress Control Number: 2021944420
First paperback printing, 2024
Paperback ISBN 978-0-691-23273-7
Cloth ISBN 978-0-691-20179-5
ISBN (e-book) 978-0-691-21121-3

British Library Cataloging-in-Publication Data is available

Editorial: Matt Rohal
Production Editorial: Jill Harris
Text Design: Karl Spurzem
Jacket/Cover Design: Jason Anscomb
Production: Erin Suydam
Publicity: Maria Whelan and Carmen Jimenez
Copyeditor: Karen Verde

Jacket/Cover art: *Labyrinth*, 2012, © Motoi Yamamoto. Bellevue Arts
Museum, Bellevue, WA

This book has been composed in ArnoPro

The great secret of death, and perhaps its deepest connection with us, is this: that, in taking from us a being we have loved and venerated, death does not wound us without, at the same time, lifting us toward a more perfect understanding of this being and of ourselves.

—RAINER MARIA RILKE, LETTER TO COUNTESS
MARGOT SIZZO-NORIS-CROUY (1923)

CONTENTS

CONTENTS

ACKNOWLEDGMENTS

Because philosophy has a long historical lineage, philosophers nearly always have to engage with many predecessors. But grief has had a relatively marginal place within philosophy, and as a result, writing this book offered me the distinct pleasure of being able to philosophize more "in the wild" than normal, developing and articulating my thoughts without being compelled to constantly situate them against the views of countless interlocutors.

That said, many of my contemporaries have lent their talents and energies to improving my own thinking and helping bring this book to fruition. Among those with whom I have profitably discussed philosophical questions related to grief are David Adams, Mahrad Almotahari, Roman Altshuler, Kathy Behrendt, John Danaher, John Davis, Guy Fletcher, James Kruger, Hugh LaFollette, Cathy Legg, Berislav Marusic, Sean McAleer, Dan Moller, Emer O'Hagan, Amy Olberding, Erica Preston-Roedder, Ryan Preston-Roedder, Matthew Ratcliffe, Michael Ridge, Peter Ross, Katie Stockdale, Patrick Stokes, Dale Turner, and Jukka Varelius. Cecilea Mun organized an author-meets-critics event, sponsored by the Society for the Philosophy of Emotion, on a draft of the manuscript. Aaron Ben Ze'ev, Purushottama Bilimoria, Dave Beisecker, Carolyn Garland, and Travis Timmerman provided extensive commentary in connection with that event.

Many of the ideas and arguments I put forth here have benefitted from feedback at public lectures and workshops. I am grateful to audiences at Cal Poly Pomona, Deakin University, the Hasting Center, Kutztown State University, Occidental College, the University of Redlands, the University of Saskatchewan, and the University of Turku for their thoughtful questions and feedback. I also thank participants at a number of professional conferences for their assistance, including the Three Rivers Philosophy Conference at the University of South Carolina (2013), the Southern California Philosophy Conference (2013), the Western Michigan Medical Humanities Conference (2014), the Mental Illness and Power Conference at the University of Memphis (2014), and the American Philosophical Association Pacific Division Meeting (2016).

Work on this book was supported by a Faculty Award grant from the National Endowment for the Humanities (award #HB-231968–16). Kathleen Higgins and Scott LaBarge kindly wrote letters in support of my application for that award. California State Polytechnic University, Pomona supported the research that generated this book in the form of a Faculty Research, Scholarship, and Creative Activities summer grant (2014) and faculty sabbatical leave (2015).

Matt Rohal at Princeton University Press ably and enthusiastically guided this project through the editorial process.

This book is dedicated to my father, Michael Cholbi (1926–2012), who taught me about grief without ever saying its name.

INTRODUCTION

Grief tends to attract the attention of creative or inquisitive minds: The emotional turbulence caused by others' deaths is a central theme in one of the earliest known literary works, the 4,000-year-old Sumerian *Epic of Gilgamesh*. Disputes about grief, burial rites, and social honor punctuate Homer's *Iliad*. Poems of grief or mourning, whether elegiac or defiant, are found in virtually all of the world's literary traditions. Many of Shakespeare's characters are emotionally vexed by grief. Indeed, cultural interest in grief appears to have accelerated in recent years, with grief a focus of innumerable personal memoirs, streaming television series, podcasts, graphic novels, and movies. For the technologically inclined, there are now several mobile phone apps to help users understand or manage their grief.

These facts speak to the powerful human interest in grief. But to judge by the number of philosophers who have investigated it, the subject is of little interest. Grief is a bit player in the history of philosophy, meriting only passing mentions in the works of eminent philosophers while receiving sustained attention from just a few.[1] And even among those philosophers for whom philosophy is a practical pursuit, a method by which to acquire the wisdom needed to live well, grief at the deaths of those who matter to us is rarely discussed, despite its being one of life's most pivotal and defining experiences.

For almost every subject, there's a "philosophy of" that subject. Philosophers have investigated the underpinnings of virtually every other academic discipline (philosophy of chemistry, economics, history, etc.), almost every profession (philosophy of medicine, education, business, etc.), many social developments (philosophy of artificial intelligence, space exploration, video games, etc.), and our major categories of social identity (race, gender, sexuality, etc.). Seen in this light, perhaps philosophers' neglect of grief is not a coincidence: Not every subject merits philosophical attention, and philosophers have not been all that interested in grief because grief is not all that philosophically interesting.

One of my goals in this book is to illustrate that this is false. Grief is in fact *extremely* interesting from a philosophical perspective. But if so, what accounts for philosophers' relative silence on the concept? Grief is an admittedly challenging topic to investigate in a sober, academic way. Emotionally complex and seemingly idiosyncratic, grief seems difficult to understand. Beyond that, in order to understand grief, we must confront some of the more unsettling realities of human life: that our emotions can sometimes prove difficult to comprehend or manage, that the people who matter to us are impermanent, and that because of this impermanence, our relationships with others are both sources of, and threats to, our sense of security, safety, and predictability. There is, then, much to be feared both in grief and in investigating grief.

But to my eye, philosophers have often brought certain intellectual assumptions to their investigation of grief, assumptions that have led them to have an at best ambivalent relationship to grief. Thanks to these assumptions, when philosophers have turned their eyes to grief, what they frequently see is embarrassing, even fearsome. For these philosophers, grief may be inevitable, but it represents the human condition at its worst: turbulent, exposed, and pitiable.

Antipathy toward grief is a common theme among ancient Mediterranean philosophers. Greek and Roman philosophers were far more hostile toward grief than we moderns, tending to view grief as, at best, a state to be tolerated or minimized. For these philosophers, grieving others' deaths is an unruly condition, a sign that one had become overly dependent on others and lacked the rational self-control characteristic of virtuous individuals. According to the influential Roman physician Galen, grief arises from excessive or covetous desires for things or people. In his view, it's better to be rid of such desires than suffer the loss of mastery over one's emotions and comportment.[2] Grief, in this interpretation, is effeminate and pathetic.[3]

In Plato's *Republic*, Socrates acknowledges that decent people will grieve their losses but insists that they should still find their grief shameful and try to moderate its public expression. He declares grief a "sickness" calling not for "lamentation" but for "medicine."[4] Socrates argues that aspiring political leaders should not be exposed to poetry depicting the "wailings and lamentations of men of repute." Any poetry with scenes of honorable men grieving should therefore be censored, with grief instead attributed only to women and "inferior men."[5] Later, in the moving death scene in *Phaedo*, Phaedo confesses that though he and Socrates' other friends had managed to control their grief up until Socrates raised the cup of hemlock to his lips, their emotions then boiled over. Tears and wailing ensued. "I wrapped my face in my cloak and wept for myself; for it was not for him that I wept, but for my own misfortune in being deprived of such a friend." Socrates rebukes them: "What conduct is this, you strange men! I sent the women away chiefly for this very reason, that they might not behave in this absurd way."[6]

As Scott LaBarge explains, authors in this tradition understood that grief is natural, but "tended to see their own grief, past or present, as evidence of a weakness that must be overcome or an error that must be corrected."[7] The remarks of the Stoic philosopher Seneca are typical in this regard: "Let not the eyes be dry when we have lost a friend, nor let them gush. We may weep, but we must not wail."[8]

Yet, lest one think that this antipathy to grief is unique to "Western" thought, we encounter a subtler expression of it in the writings of the Chinese Daoist philosopher Zhuangzi. Zhuangzi preached acceptance of all change, including death. In one well-known parable, the Master Hui arrives to comfort Zhuangzi upon the death of his wife. Hui unexpectedly finds Zhuangzi banging on a basin and singing rather than wailing or weeping:

> Master Hui said: "You lived with her; she raised your children and grew old. Now that she is dead, it is enough that you do not weep for her; but banging on a drum and singing—is this not extreme?"
>
> Master Zhuang said: "It is not so. When she first died, how indeed could I not have been melancholy? But I considered that in the beginning, she was without life; not only was she without life, but she was originally without form; not only was she without form, but she was originally without qi.[9] . . . the qi changed, and there was form; the form changed, and there was life; and now there is another change, and there is death. This is the same as the progression of the four seasons, spring, autumn, summer, winter. Moreover, she sleeps now, reclining, in a giant chamber; if I were to have

accompanied her, weeping and wailing, I would have considered myself ignorant of destiny. So I stopped."[10]

Admittedly, Zhaungzi's parable does not echo the strident tone of Plato and other ancient Mediterranean philosophers. And at one level, Zhuangzi's counsel is sensible: We should not forget that the deaths of those we love are as inevitable as the changing of the seasons. Yet he too sees grief as foolhardy, the result (he contends) of our forgetting our human "destiny." And, like the Greeks and Romans, Zhuangzi invites the reader to try to *transcend* grief, in his case, by reminding ourselves that the lives and deaths of the loved ones for whom we grieve are but episodes within the larger cycle of nature. Zhuangzi's parable does not *condemn* grief exactly. But it does consign grief to that set of emotions we undergo only because we are unduly fixated on the ephemeral and the mutable instead of on what is durable and unchanging. Like the Greeks and Romans, Zhuangzi understands grief as a consequence of ignorance. We grieve (or grieve to excess) because we have not fully taken to heart lessons about the larger world and our place in it. Grief thus reflects negatively on those who grieve, bringing to light their human shortcomings rather than expressing their best or truest natures.

Notice that these philosophers' antipathy toward grief does not rest on any reluctance on their part to confront death. In fact, these traditions emphasize that philosophical wisdom is needed to ready us for *our own* deaths. Socrates went so far as to proclaim that philosophy just is preparation for death. Rather, what alarms these philosophers about grief is how it underscores human interdependence and our ensuing vulnerability to loss. And, while grief may shock us, this is not because, as Zhuangzi seems to allege, we are ignorant of human mortality.[11] We do not grieve because we are ignorant of human mortality; we seem rather to grieve despite knowing that humans inevitably die.

Grief, according to much of this philosophical tradition, is a source of shame. If so, then to linger over a phenomenon that reveals us in an unflattering light when we could instead try to figure out how to become the kinds of self-sufficient, invulnerable, and implacable individuals who neither can nor need to grieve does not make much sense. In this tradition, grief is a personal deficiency to be overcome instead of a philosophical problem whose depths should be plumbed.

Nowadays, philosophers do not seem to share the ancient conviction that grief is shameful. Nevertheless, a certain hesitancy about too openly acknowledging grief, or opening up grief to public philosophical scrutiny, is visible in a more recent episode in which a philosopher could *not* avoid grief.

In the summer of 1960, the British writer and theologian C. S. Lewis was sixty-one years old and at the peak of his professional and intellectual acclaim. Six years earlier, he had been appointed as the first holder of a newly established chair in medieval and renaissance literature at Cambridge University. His BBC radio broadcasts in the early 1940s, when London had been subject to repeated Nazi bombings, had been published as *Mere Christianity*. That work, along with essays such as *Miracles* and *The Problem of Pain* and the epistolary novel *The Screwtape Letters*, had made Lewis arguably the world's foremost spokesperson for Christianity. His works for children were also wildly popular; his seven-part series of novels, *The Chronicles of Narnia*, would eventually sell more than 100 million copies.

But professional acclaim would soon collide with private turmoil.

Four years earlier, Lewis had married the American poet Joy Davidman. His attraction had intellectual roots: Davidman had won multiple awards for her poetry and had authored a scholarly interpretation of the Ten Commandments for which Lewis had written the preface. But their love went beyond the cerebral. Lewis would write that Joy "was my daughter and my mother, my pupil and my teacher, my subject and my sovereign . . . my trusty comrade, friend, shipmate, fellow-soldier." Only a few months into their marriage, Joy broke her leg, treatment for which revealed that she had developed cancer. The diagnosis seemed only to catalyze Lewis's growing affection for her. The years from 1957, when Joy's cancer went into remission, to 1959, when it returned, appear to be the most joyful in Lewis's adult life. In April 1960, Joy and "Jack" (as Lewis was known to his familiars) took a holiday to Greece, fulfilling Joy's lifelong wish to see the Aegean Sea.

And then, on July 13, Joy died.

Jack Lewis was not the sort of person to be unprepared for life's challenges: Both of his parents had died of cancer, his mother when he was but nine years old. Jack moved from Ireland to England as a teenager, saw combat in World War I, lost and regained his Christian faith in early adulthood, and took in children evacuated from the London blitz.

But to judge from the journals he kept in the days following Joy's death, Jack was caught hopelessly unprepared for his own grief.[12]

Jack was embarrassed by the tears and sorrow, but at least he had anticipated them. What he had not expected was how "grief felt so like fear."[13] Nor had he expected his grief to include feelings of mild drunkenness (like being "concussed"), distraction and boredom ("I find it hard to take in what anyone says. . . . It is so uninteresting"), or isolation and alienation ("There is a sort of invisible blanket between the world and me"). Nor had anyone warned him about how grief induces languor or "laziness."

> I loathe the slightest effort. Not only writing but even reading a letter is too much. Even shaving. What does it matter now whether my cheek is rough or smooth?[14]

Grief had made Jack a stranger to himself. His own body was foreign to him, an "empty house" where he felt Joy's absence most acutely.[15] A shared Christian faith had bound him to Joy, but it too did not seem up to the task of helping Jack find his way after her death. Instead, Joy's absence sparked the only crisis of faith he had undergone since his conversion three decades earlier. "Meanwhile," Jack asked, "where is God?"[16]

For devotees of Lewis's work, the Jack Lewis of the early chapters of A Grief Observed likely comes as a surprise. They probably would not have predicted that Joy's death would transform Lewis from an articulate public intellectual and Christian apologist to a frightened and bewildered man with wavering faith, a distracted mind, and a fractured sense of self. Readers may well have been taken aback by Lewis's grief, struggling to reconcile it with his plea elsewhere to "submit to death, death of your ambitions and favorite wishes every day and death of your whole body, in the end submit with every fiber of your being."[17]

Lewis himself would die three years later. But in the interim, he considered whether to publish the journals cataloguing his own grief experience. For reasons that remain murky, he was reluctant for the journals to be associated with him. An apparent compromise was struck; the journals were published a year later as *A Grief Observed*, but under the pseudonym N. W. Clerk, and with Joy referred to simply as "H."

We cannot know for certain exactly what lies behind Lewis's trepidation about publishing his grief journals. As a trained philosopher, Lewis was no doubt well versed in the philosophical tradition to which I earlier referred, a tradition in which grief is an embarrassment to be overcome. We can detect in *A Grief Observed*, and Lewis's decision to publish it posthumously and pseudonymously, an inkling of such embarrassment. While he could not avoid grief in his private life, he managed to avoid it in his *public* life. For, while readers later learn of Jack's grief, Lewis died having shielded it from public scrutiny. In this respect, Lewis's life story embodies the tradition of philosophical antipathy toward grief: Whatever the private significance of grief, it is too shameful to be a subject of proper public philosophy.

But why should grief elicit shame? Is it possible to acknowledge that even though grief sometimes *causes* shame, such shame is improper, an echo of mistaken beliefs about what grief is and what it says about us?

By shrinking from grief as a subject of sustained inquiry, philosophers have not had to confront a potent counterexample to deeply held convictions about what is possible and desirable for us. Ironically then, these convictions have impeded full, non-dogmatic philosophical inquiry into grief. After all, grief only appears shameful and philosophically uninteresting *if* we accept the view that grief is bad and should be avoided. But should we accept these claims? Honest and sustained attention to grief itself may well cast these into doubt. In other words, get close enough to grief and not only will antipathy toward it dissolve but the worldview that marginalizes grief as a philosophical subject may waver as well. Ultimately, we avoid what we fear. Much of the philosophical tradition thus seems to fear grief for what it might say about us human beings. Specifically, to investigate grief with the same probity and exactitude philosophers bring to other subjects may bring to light a possibility that many may fear—to wit, that our finitude, vulnerability, and interdependence neither can be nor should be fully overcome.

———

I have not had a particularly difficult go of things grief-wise. With just more than half of my expected life in the books, I have had my share of grief, and have found it mildly distressing but far from tortuous. Certainly, Jack Lewis's grief at Joy's death was far more intense than anything I have undergone.

At its best, philosophy is courageous and practical. Its historical avoidance of grief is neither. To avoid grief for fear of entertaining uncomfortable questions about the human condition is not courageous. And neglecting one of the most distinctively human and life-defining events we face is not practical. One of philosophy's greatest uses is in helping us navigate life's more bewildering transitions: maturation, parenthood, romantic love, aging, death. In that light, our philosophical neglect of grief is faintly scandalous. We can certainly do better.

Yet the fact that philosophers have largely neglected grief does not show that there is much to be gained by investigating grief in a philosophical way. One might be skeptical that philosophy has any distinctive contribution to make to our knowledge of grief because other disciplines and practices have already shone the spotlight on it. Perhaps we need guidance about grief, but no *philosophical* guidance about grief.

I certainly do not think philosophy has a monopoly on understanding grief. But it does have a distinctive role to play that cannot be fulfilled by other disciplines or forms of expertise.

For instance, grief has been extensively studied by psychologists and psychiatrists. I will often reference their work in this book because the conclusions philosophers reach about some phenomenon should at least be compatible with the best evidence other disciplines provide about that same phenomenon. Philosophy need not compete with the answers provided by other disciplines. It can instead address questions that other disciplines are ill-equipped to answer. A philosophical understanding of grief should therefore accord with what psychologists, etc., have discovered about the grief experience. Still, there are two reasons psychology is not likely to offer compelling answers to certain questions we are likely to have about grief. First, psychology studies the workings of our minds— what is "in our heads." I will have a lot to say in this book about the psychology of grief, but focusing on grief as a purely mental phenomenon overlooks the non-mental facts involved in grief. As we shall see, grief occurs because of our ties to other people as well as our ties to our own past and future selves. Grief is thus about *how our minds relate to the wider world*, a consideration that purely psychological approaches to grief may shortchange. Second, psychology aims to be a descriptive discipline, discovering the laws that govern our thoughts and experiences. But many of our questions about grief are not descriptive in nature. They are instead ethical questions about why we should care about grief, whether we should be glad (rather than resentful) that we grieve, or whether grief is morally obligatory. Such questions are philosophical in nature.

Similarly, health care providers are often the first resource we turn to in order to address life challenges, and we might therefore hope to answer these questions about grief by turning to mental health professionals. Recent decades have witnessed an explosive growth in the grief counseling industry. It is certainly not the purpose of this book to disparage grief counseling. No doubt many bereaved persons benefit from it. But the "therapeutic" challenges grief raises for us do not seem necessarily medical in nature.[18] I will offer explicit arguments against viewing grief as a medical problem later (in chapter 7). But for now, suffice to say that some of the challenges grief presents are "problems in living," problems arising not because our lives have gone wrong somehow but because human life has certain predicaments baked into it. And philosophy is often where we turn for help with those predicaments.

Literature and the arts also can no doubt be instructive with regard to grief.[19] This book contains many references to grief memoirs and other literary works that illustrate claims about grief that we also have nonliterary reasons to accept. Yet no single artistic work can fully illuminate grief's nuances. For one, such works nearly always focus on a single grief episode. We can learn a great deal about grief when such episodes are representative of grief experience in general, but if they are atypical, they are as likely to mislead as to inform. Also keep in mind that literature and the arts thrive on drama and are thus likely to overrepresent the most intense or emotionally high-pitched grief episodes at the expense of representations of ordinary, more "healthy" grief episodes.[20] Shakespeare's Hamlet, for instance, vividly exemplifies how grief can simultaneously feel inescapable and enigmatic. But (fortunately) only a fraction of bereaved people ultimately contemplate suicide (as Hamlet seems to), and only a smaller fraction of the bereaved are thereby led to violence.

The Internet blogosphere is also saturated with advice on how to deal with grief. But much of it suffers from the same defect as artistic depictions of grief, drawing solely upon the blogger's experience while neglecting the voluminous scientific research on the subject. In other cases, Internet resources largely add to the haze that surrounds grief by devolving to a tired therapeutic language of "closure," "healing," and "journeys," which lacks philosophical mettle.

More generally, grief is a serious matter that deserves to be taken seriously, but we are only rarely invited to *understand* grief. And as I will elaborate later in chapter 3, in addition to involving painful emotions, grief is also made more difficult by the fact that it is often a bewildering experience. We often seem not to grasp what happens to us when we grieve. When successful, philosophy provides us just such an understanding.

In fact, that understanding requires a philosophical *theory* of grief. If that word "theory" sends shivers down your spine, be assured that I don't have in mind anything weighty. If we are to understand grief, we need to understand its various facets, considering both what various grief experiences have in common as well as how they differ. A good theory unifies what we know about some domain, so that we see how these different parcels of knowledge interrelate. And in the case of grief, we have many philosophical insights but not, to my mind, a well-developed theory. My hope is that the theory outlined in this book enables us to see grief clearly, both in its parts and as a whole.

Still, you might doubt that a philosophical theory of grief can do much to alleviate the *emotional* tumult of grief. Admittedly, a rich philosophical understanding of grief may lessen the confusion that can surround it. But that understanding is helpless in the face of the agony of grief. Above all else, we seek comfort when thinking about grief, and philosophy is unlikely to comfort us.

To be clear, even the best philosophical theory of grief almost certainly cannot solve every challenge grief presents to us. But we should not underestimate how important understanding grief is to the task of negotiating its emotional shoals. We are better off knowing the truth about grief than finding comfort in half-truths and platitudes. Ultimately, each of us wants to live in light of the truth, however jarring the truth might be. The greatest and most lasting comfort is found in the truth. Lewis himself put it well:

> [C]omfort is the one thing you cannot get by looking for it. If you look for truth, you may find comfort in the end: if you look for comfort you will not get either comfort or truth— only soft soap and wishful thinking to begin with and, in the end, despair.[21]

Hence, everyone stands to benefit from this book insofar as they can benefit from a more robust philosophical understanding of one of life's "big emotions."

That said, some will benefit more than others. In particular, this book is not principally aimed at those *in the midst of* grief. The emotional throes of grief may make it difficult to think about grief with the degree of detachment philosophy often requires. Moreover, as we shall learn in chapter 2, grief typically makes great demands on our attention, to the degree that it can compromise our ability to concentrate and to retain working memories.[22] I have sought to make my theory as accessible as possible to those with little philosophical background. Still, philosophy is a demanding enterprise and, as such, those in the midst of the cognitive fog of grief may struggle to engage fully with our philosophical inquiry.

However, this inquiry is likely to be more beneficial to those for whom grief has waned. The experience of grief teaches us about grief, but some questions can linger. More fundamentally, I would like to show those who have grieved exactly why it can be a benefit—why, in the end, our propensity for grief should be welcomed rather than regretted.

I also intend this inquiry to benefit us prospectively, in *advance of* grief. As I have indicated, this book is not meant to be therapeutic in the usual way. But one way philosophy can be therapeutic is by readying us for what is to come. In particular, I hope that this inquiry can dispel the fear that I suspect grief often evokes. Earlier I criticized the philosophical tradition for being afraid of what grief might say about us. That fear may be ill-founded, but that does not mean there is nothing to be feared in grief. Grief can result from events (the deaths of those close to you) that we have reason to fear, as well as being harrowing in its own right. In particular, grief can induce in us a frightening sense of helplessness, of being tossed about in an emotional seastorm. But the likelihood of grief in our lifetimes is high, and if we shrink from trying to understand grief because we are afraid to look it square in the eye, we bar ourselves from the one path to addressing this fear. Fear of uncertainty and of the unknown are arguably among our greatest fears, after all. I doubt I can make the case that you should look forward to grief, exactly. All the same, knowing grief as well as we can in advance of grieving can diminish our fear of an event that we will not, in all likelihood, be able to avoid.

This book thus fits into a tradition that sees one of philosophy's key tasks as that of *consolation*, of helping us navigate our expectations for our lives, particularly by enabling us to understand ourselves and our circumstances. The grief we undergo in response to the deaths of those who matter to us represents a circumstance that is difficult to avoid and yet poses a challenge to what we expect, or hope for, from the world. Addressing these challenges, I will try to illustrate in this book, is best done through a richer understanding of their nature and of ourselves.

My hope is that this book will *not* be the last word from philosophers on grief. Every philosopher of course wants to be right. But influencing philosophical discourse is no less valuable. The centrality of grief to the human experience makes it ripe for philosophical investigation, so the paucity of philosophical attention it has received is lamentable. Perhaps the account of grief and its importance expounded here, even if mistaken, will persuade philosophers that the subject deserves better.

————

Before our inquiry begins, let me provide a chapter-by-chapter preview of what is to come. For those who are eager to jump right in, feel free to move ahead.

The deaths of others elicit a range of responses from us. Anyone with a semblance of moral sensitivity is at least mildly dismayed upon learning of the deaths of others. However, only *some* of our responses to others count as grief responses. Chapter 1 takes up the question of how grief is differentiated from other responses to the deaths of others by addressing the *scope* of grief: For which individuals do we grieve? What must be true of another person, or of our relationship to her, such that her death is a loss that elicits grief? In this chapter, I argue that we grieve for those in whom we have invested our *practical identities*, that is, we grieve those who come to play crucial roles in our aspirations and commitments—indeed, in how we understand ourselves and in what we find valuable or worthwhile in our lives. This claim helps explain grief such as Jack Lewis's— the grief we feel at the deaths of close loved ones or family members—but also grief prompted by the deaths of those with whom we lack that same intimacy or familiarity, such as artists, politicians, or other public figures.

To know who we grieve for is still not to say what grief is. Chapter 2 develops a philosophical account of grief's nature. Specifically, I argue first that grief, unlike emotions such as fear and anger, is a series of affective states rather than a single such state. Elisabeth Kübler-Ross popularized this notion with her well-known "five stage" model, wherein grief progresses through denial, anger, bargaining, depression, and acceptance. Subsequent research has found that Kübler-Ross's model is correct at a broad level but often gets the details of grief wrong: Grief typically includes multiple distinct emotions, but many of us do not undergo these five emotional stages, do not undergo them in this order (unsurprisingly, acceptance usually comes first), or undergo other emotions besides these five (guilt, fear, confusion, etc.). Second, I argue that grief should be thought of as a kind of emotionally driven *attention*. Grief responds to the deaths of others, not by immediately disclosing their importance but by motivating us to take notice of their deaths and interrogate how those deaths matter to us. Finally, although grieving is not a process we can dictate, it is nevertheless an *activity* that responds to our choices and actions and that has a discernible aim. These three features of grief qua emotion (that it is a process, a kind of attention, and an activity) as well as the conclusions regarding the scope of grief defended in chapter 1, suggest that grief's object—what grief is ultimately *about*—is the bereaved individual's relationship with the deceased, a relationship that invariably has been transformed by the latter's death.

Our exploration then turns to several foundational ethical questions concerning grief. Chapters 3 and 4 address what I believe to be the principal ethical quandary caused by grief: Grief is by its nature painful or distressing, but also seems capable of contributing to our overall well-being. Many individuals are even drawn to the painful aspects of bereavement, in fact. This tension is the *paradox of grief*. Chapter 3 proposes that, because grief involves sustained and diverse emotional attention to an integral relationship whose terms must change due to the death of one of its participants, grief is uniquely situated to afford us self-knowledge, and in particular, knowledge of the values, emotional dispositions, and concerns that make up what I call our practical identities. The deaths of those to whom we are attached trigger, to a greater or lesser degree, a "crisis" in our relationship to them, which in turn generates a crisis in our own identity. It does this by highlighting that our values, commitments, and concerns are not simply "givens" that can be taken for granted but are dependent on relationships with other mortal beings. When they die, our relationships with them can—indeed *must*—change. The challenge of figuring out how those relationships shall change is the central puzzle grief provides. We solve this challenge when our grieving results in valuable self-knowledge.

This argument establishes how grief can be good for us despite its being painful or distressing. However, this argument does not fully explain why individuals often *seek out* opportunities to undergo painful grief experiences. Chapter 4 argues that while such experiences are genuinely painful, such experiences can be desirable as indispensable components of a larger valuable activity (in the way that, say, pain experienced in the course of strenuous exercise can be desirable insofar as it is inherent to an activity that is valuable overall).

A second foundational ethical question about grief is whether it is rational. Chapter 5 argues against two views that deny the possibility of rational grief. The first posits that grief is *arational*, not subject to rational appraisal at all. The second posits that grief is *necessarily irrational*. I propose that grief is *contingently rational*. The rationality of grief is primarily retrospective, to be judged based on how well a grief episode and the emotions that embody it reflect the significance of the relationship the bereaved had with the deceased. A rational grief episode, on my view, is both qualitatively and quantitatively appropriate to that loss. In other words, *our grieving is rational when we feel the right emotions in the right degree in light of the loss of the relationship with the deceased that we have suffered.* The chapter concludes by arguing that although grief can be (and often is) rational in this respect, grieving individuals are nevertheless prone to irrationality when they are asked to make decisions regarding the dead or dying person for whom they grieve.

Chapter 6 considers whether, as the late Robert Solomon proposed, there is a duty to grieve. Those who do not grieve, or grieve without apparently sufficient depth or intensity, are open to apparent moral blame. I argue that such a duty is misunderstood if classified either as a duty owed to those who grieve the same deaths as we do or as a duty owed to the deceased. Neither of these duties reflect the essentially egocentric nature of grief defended in chapters 1 and 2. Instead, the best candidate for a duty to grieve is that it is self-regarding, i.e., a duty to oneself. Echoing the conclusions of chapter 3, the duty to grieve rests on a duty to pursue substantial self-knowledge—knowledge of one's own values, dispositions, for example—so as to render rational the pursuit of one's conception of the good. The duty to grieve thus belongs to the duties stemming from a moral requirement to respect and perfect ourselves as rational agents.

Chapter 7 addresses grief in the context of mental health and the treatment thereof. As noted earlier, ancient philosophers worried that grief portended a loss of reason or self-control. Such worries fit into a long-standing cultural pattern depicting grief as a species of madness. Questions about grief and mental disorder came into public view about a decade ago when a committee developing a new version of the *Diagnostic and Statistical Manual of Mental Disorders* suggested changing the status of grief, jettisoning the claim that grief (despite having much in common with recognized mental disorders such as depression) is a "normal" response to loss and proposing the introduction of a new "complicated grief disorder." Denunciations of these moves to "medicalize" grief were swift. This chapter argues that while mental health treatment is sometimes appropriate in the course of grief, grief's medicalization should be resisted. While grief often resembles mental disorders in diminishing our sense of well-being and hampering our ability to function day-to-day, it nearly always represents a healthy response to others' death—a sign of good underlying mental health rather than a pathology. A grieving person can of course be ill and therefore an appropriate subject of medical attention. But even when illness has grief as its source, the individual is almost never *sick with grief*. Normalizing the medical treatment of grief would do more harm than good.

CHAPTER ONE

For Whom We Grieve

According to the US Central Intelligence Agency, about 55 million human beings die each year. That works out to about 152,000 deaths each day, 6,300 per hour, 105 each minute, and two each second.[1]

I imagine that you do not grieve many of these deaths. (I readily concede that I only grieve a miniscule handful of them.) Of course, others' deaths—even those we do not grieve—can elicit other emotional responses in us besides grief. We are outraged when we hear of a vicious killing or of the killing of an especially vulnerable person. We are horrified upon learning about acts of genocide. And we can pity the deaths of those who are close to those we know (as when we learn that a friend's parent has died).

Many of these are deaths that we *mourn*. Sometimes mourning and grief are viewed as the same phenomenon. But, although they are connected, they are nevertheless distinct. Grief, as we shall understand it, is the specific and personal emotional reaction individuals have to other individuals' deaths. At its core, it is a psychological phenomenon. Grief is what happens "inside" us as we react to a death of someone who matters to us. The ways in which we grasp and describe grief are not private, since they are the product of acculturation. But the phenomenon itself is private at its core. Mourning, in contrast, is more public and often ritualistic. Many of those who are mourning are also grieving. In fact, mourning is a common *way* to grieve. In those instances, mourning is the public or behavioral face of grieving. But it is possible to mourn—to participate in memorials, say, or observe a moment of silence for the deceased—without grieving. Throughout human history, there have been professional mourners. It is possible to pay someone to mourn precisely because mourning involves engaging in a set of behaviors. Paying someone to grieve, on the other hand, appears incoherent because there is no way for monetary incentives to induce the private psychological state of grief. No amount of money can motivate someone to care about the deaths of a particular person in the way that a bereaved person cares about the death of that person. Paying others to grieve is thus no more possible than paying someone else to have fun for you or to sleep for you.

Hence, while there may be something ethically deficient about a person who reacts with complete indifference to the deaths of other people, there is nothing ethically deficient about a person who grieves only rarely.[2] For it seems to belong to the nature of grief that it is a selective response. We neither can nor should grieve all deaths of others. Every human life matters, and so every human death matters. But not every human life matters (equally) to us as individuals, and so not every human death matters (equally) to us as individuals. Thus, unlike the reactions that others' deaths usually elicit in us, grief is fundamentally self-focused. To be outraged at a vicious murder is to feel rage on behalf of the victim or those who cared about her. To pity another grieving person is to feel sorrow at what has befallen her. Grief, in contrast, is what happens when another's death is meaningful directly for the bereaved.

We thus grieve when and because the death of another person is particularly or acutely significant for us. I will refer to this as the *egocentric* aspect of grief. Note that this term does not imply that grief is selfish. Grief, I shall argue in this book, is self-concerning, and in a broad sense of the term, self-interested. Grief *can* matter to how our lives go. But it is not objectionably self-interested to grieve. A person shows herself no undue favor or partiality by grieving.

We do not grieve all deaths, nor (I contend) ought we grieve all deaths. For, in order to grieve a person's death, there must be some distinctive tie or connection we bear to the deceased. Our challenge in this chapter is therefore to identify the sort of relationship a grieving person must have with the deceased for their grief to be intelligible. We will first consider three apparently plausible accounts of how a person must be related to a deceased individual in order for grief to be intelligible. These accounts succeed in making sense of fairly typical cases of grief. However, they come up short in explaining grief in more atypical cases that are nevertheless true instances of grief. I then defend my own account of the relationship needed for grief, one that rests on *identity investment*. This account, I suggest, successfully explains both typical and atypical cases of grief.

1. Intimacy

A first possibility for the relationship that grief requires is that the bereaved must be *intimate* with the deceased. Our stereotypical cases of grief certainly are those in which intimacy exists between the bereaved and the deceased. The characteristic marks of intimacy—warmth, familiarity, knowledge of another person's attitudes and day-to-day habits—are present in the circumstances where grief is likely to be particularly intense, for example, the deaths of a spouse, a child, or a close sibling. Such relationships may be the ones for which grief is potentially most important or valuable. This intimacy need not be reciprocal in order for grief to occur. For instance, it seems clear that prospective parents (and mothers in particular) grieve the deaths of fetuses that are miscarried. Although fetuses do not have habits, attitudes, personalities, etc., as robust as newborns, children, or adults, parents nevertheless have a kind of intimacy with these fetuses rooted in the experience of conception, gestation, and preparation for childbirth.[3] Presumably, however, the fetuses lack the sophisticated mental life needed to be intimate with their parents.

While intimacy is often present in the relationships we have with those whose deaths we grieve, intimacy does not appear to be a *defining* feature of the relationships for which the death of another prompts grief. For individuals can grieve for deceased persons whom they hardly knew or who were effectively strangers to them. The rise of social media makes it apparent that many people experience grief at the deaths of public figures they did not know personally, such as artists, musicians, athletes, or political leaders. If these are genuine instances of grief—and there is no reason not to take them at face value—then intimacy is not required in any meaningful sense to grieve another's death.

It is tempting to say that grief for public figures is not *really* grief for them because their admirers or fans do not know the public figures well enough to grieve them. In this case, those who grieve the deaths of public figures are undergoing authentic grief, but they are grieving the public figures, not the full-blooded individuals. Those who grieved John F. Kennedy's assassination were grieving Kennedy the war hero and president, not the man whose day-to-day life they were not privy to; those who grieved

the death of pop star David Bowie were grieving Bowie (or perhaps his several stage personas), not the person known to his
family and friends. This suggestion is plausible. Admittedly, in
today's information- saturated media environment, it may be
possible to achieve a minimal level of intimacy with public figures. A person who read Nelson Mandela's autobiographical
books, followed his activities in the news, and so on, appeared to
know enough about him to grieve for something more than
merely his public persona. Still, the focus of the grief felt for a
deceased public figure is on their public personas—their accom-
plishments, observable personality traits and values, for
example—such that there necessarily exists a gap between that
persona and the individual for whom a public figure's friends or
family would grieve.

But this suggestion does not support the claim that grief for
public figures is somehow a counterfeit or less than fully realized form of grief. It instead underscores the perils of taking
what are arguably our paradigm cases of grief—grief for those
with whom we share personal intimacy—as demarcating the
scope of whom we can grieve for. No doubt the role played in
one's life by one's spouse is different from the role played by
one's favorite jazz artist or a well-known human rights activist.
Yet this difference merely entails that we can and should grieve
our spouses differently from how we grieve jazz artists or
human rights activists, not that the latter group cannot or
should not be grieved by those who lacked intimacy with
them. Indeed, it is striking how *little* intimacy is needed to trigger grief at another's death. Consider an adult adopted as a
child who was notified only of his birth mother's name and had
no contact with her throughout his life. It does not strain imagination, in my opinion, to suppose that the adult child could
grieve upon learning of the birth mother's death despite the

utter lack of knowledge or intimacy he had with the birth mother. (We could even describe this as grief for the "imagined" mother.[4]) As we shall discuss later in this chapter, such an example illustrates that grief may be less about personal realities than about personal aspirations.

2. Love

A second possibility for the relationship needed to ground grief is that we grieve those whom we *love*. I will not make any pretense here of trying to untangle the thorny philosophical questions about love. But a philosophical account of love is not necessary to grasp why this proposal will not suffice for delineating the scope of grief. For one, some of the counterexamples offered against the claim that grief requires intimacy also apply here. It strains credulity to suppose that those who grieve public figures literally love them. Love their music, their art, their political stances, their athletic prowess? Yes. But the admiration, reverence, or envy we feel for public figures need not rise to the level of love.

Indeed, we need not even *like* those whose deaths we grieve. Fidel Castro was the target of forty-two assassination schemes by the Kennedy administration, but Kennedy's death reportedly caused Castro sadness. Enemies or rivals can therefore grieve each other.

That grief presupposes love also runs headlong into the fact that grief can be prompted by the deaths of those we *hate*. It is often noted that grief can involve ambivalent feelings. Not every instance of ambivalent grief occurs because the bereaved individual's relationship with the deceased was itself ambivalent. But grief can nevertheless occur when a person about whom we have conflicted, even hateful, feelings dies. A person can be a source of disappointment or indignation and yet still be grieved upon their death. Children are known to grieve parents who abused or even abandoned them. Grief is incompatible with indifference, but compatible with both love *and* hate. At the very least, we should not be quick to dismiss grief that is tinged with emotional ambivalence toward the deceased.

3. Attachment

A third possibility is that grief arises when a person dies to whom we stand in a relationship of *attachment*. For a person to be attached to an individual is to relate to them in the following ways:

i. The attached person longs to be proximate to, and to interact with, that individual.

ii. Upon separation from that individual, the attached person tends to experience distress.

iii. The attached person feels secure in the presence of the individual to whom she is attached.

iv. Only the individual to whom she is attached instantiates features i–iii in precisely the way she does.[5]

That grief requires attachment to the deceased is a promising hypothesis. It helps explain the egocentric character of grief. For if we grieve those to whom we are attached, it would not be at all surprising for us to experience their deaths as a loss due to the unique emotional dependence we have on them. Their deaths would portend a decrease in our sense of security that no other person could compensate for. Moreover, as we shall see in chapter 2, grief can include many different emotional states, including anxiety, which is to be expected if attachment is what determines who we grieve for.

Here again, though, we must be mindful of mistaking typical cases of grief for all cases of grief. Several of the examples of grief adduced thus far do not seem to involve especially rich attachment on the part of the bereaved toward the deceased. Those who grieve public figures or who grieve biological parents they never met are not attached to those deceased individuals. Similarly, parents grieve the deaths of fetuses who are electively aborted. Yet it seems unlikely that such parents are emotionally reliant upon those fetuses. Furthermore, grief can often occur when the deceased were attached to the bereaved rather than vice versa. No doubt many parents are attached to their children; they feel distress in their absence, long to be near them, view them as irreplaceable. But not every parent is emotionally dependent on their children in the way captured by the notion of attachment. They may enjoy their children's company, for example, without its being true that the absence of their children causes them insecurity or distress.

4. Well-Being

That grief requires intimacy with, love of, or attachment to the deceased each proves inadequate. These accounts overlook certain kinds of relationships in which grief is possible or mistake the features of the most familiar or most vivid species of grief for features of grief as such. In rejecting these accounts of whom we grieve for, I do not at all intend that intimacy, love, or attachment are irrelevant to grief. As we shall see in later chapters, how we grieve—and how we *ought* to grieve—depends crucially on the nature of the relationship we have (or had) with the person whose death prompts our grief. We do not, and ought not to, grieve our spouses as we do our deceased siblings, our professional colleagues as we do our spiritual role models, our athletic heroes as we do our longtime neighbors. Grief should be as variegated as the kinds of relationships human beings can have to one another, which is to say, highly variegated. But that still leaves the task of identifying the features needed for one's relationship with a deceased individual to elicit grief (as opposed to other reactions, such as sorrow, pity, and so on).

In order to progress toward identifying these features, recall the egocentric aspect of grief I mentioned earlier. Grief, unlike other reactions we have to others' deaths, is egocentric inasmuch as their deaths are particularly or acutely significant to ourselves. One way in which another's death can result in a significant loss to us is that we lose the various goods that the person provided us while they were alive. The death of a friend means the loss of companionship; a colleague, a source of professional support or inspiration; a spouse, romantic love and shared life goals. Grief can feel like a painful wound because it responds to a threat to our well-being. We thus grieve the deaths of those who contribute to our well-being.

This line of thought is promising, but overstated. As noted earlier, we do not only grieve for those who make our lives better. We can also grieve for those who bitterly disappoint us. We can also grieve those with whom we did not have a lengthy enough relationship for them to contribute much to our well-being. For example, parents grieve for miscarried children, and it would not be surprising for a person to grieve the death of someone whom she had fallen in love with only the day before. In these cases, the bereaved are not prompted to grieve by what the deceased *actually* contributed to their well-being. They instead seem to grieve for those whom they *hoped* (or had once hoped) would contribute significantly to their well-being, even if they did not, either due to happenstance or personal failure.

Such observations illustrate that the connection between grief and well-being is more complex than it appears. We do grieve for those whom we recognize as contributing (or as having contributed) to our well-being. But we also grieve for those whose actions, choices, and attitudes, have not borne on, or that we see as having no bearing on, our well-being. Another's death prompts us to grieve when that person occupies an identifiable place within how we understand our concerns, our lives, and ourselves.

5. Being Invested in the Dead

As I shall put it, what unites all those for whom we grieve is what I call *practical identity investment*. Each of us embraces some set of commitments, values, and concerns. This set guides most all our choices and actions. It includes those things that matter to us in more than a momentary or fleeting way. In this respect, these commitments, values, and concerns help to give shape and direction to our lives. We invoke them to explain why we make pivotal life choices, to give an accounting of ourselves when others misunderstand or question what we do, and to give our lives a measure of integrity. Such commitments, values, and concerns thus serve to define us, not so much in a metaphysical sense—telling us what our nature is—but in a practical sense, telling us (and the world) what it is about us that makes us valuable and worthy of the attention and energy we tend to direct at ourselves. In the absence of any such commitments, values, or concerns, our *investment* in ourselves becomes inscrutable and, seemingly, groundless. Without them, we are deprived of the resources needed to make sense of ourselves as practical beings, as active beings for whom reasons serve to justify our choices.

Christine Korsgaard has coined the useful term "practical identity" for this set of commitments, values, and concerns. Korsgaard emphasizes that a person's practical identity consists of more than her values. It also provides the foundation of what we value in and about ourselves. Your practical identity, she writes, is "a description under which you value yourself, a description under which you find your life to be worth living and your actions to be worth undertaking."[6] Crucially, many of the elements of our practical identities are commitments, values, and concerns that necessarily involve others and their practical identities. Korsgaard observes that among the elements of practical identities are "roles and relationships, citizenship, memberships in ethnic or religious groups, causes, vocations, professions, and offices."[7] Many other individuals will therefore play indispensable roles in our practical identities; as such, our practical identities would be impossible or incoherent without them. Of course, different individuals play different parts in our practical identities. Role models, even those we do not know intimately, may shape our practical identities by helping us figure out what we care about. Others—for example, our spouses or romantic partners—play a role in our practical identities by being objects of love, by sharing values or goals with us, and by caring for us. Some of our commitments or goals only make sense if there are rivals or enemies who stand in the way of their realization. Thus, our practical identities are, in a diversity of ways, *invested* in the existence of others. We grieve a person's death—and it is *appropriate* that we grieve a person's death—to the extent that our practical identities are invested in their existence. The more central another person is to our practical identity, the greater cause we have for grieving them upon their deaths.

Because identity investment comes in degrees, our susceptibility to grief, and grief itself, comes in degrees. There is probably no "bright line" to be drawn between those we can (and ought to) grieve and those we cannot (and ought not to) grieve.

But some individuals will exercise disproportionate influence on our self-understanding and our practical identities. It is for them that grief is most apt.

Imagine that a person's biography is being written by an expert observer. This biography would, by necessity, have to mention the various relationships in a person's life. But taken in the broadest sense of the term "relationship," we have a wide range of relationships—not only with friends and family, but also with our plumber, our tax accountant, and so on. And in trying to compose a person's life story, an expert biographer would not give equal priority to all of these relationships, for some of these relationships are far more central to how the subject of the biography understood herself and her life. These relationships, the identity-constituting relationships, are those whose omission from the expert's biography would render it incomplete. Without attention to such relationships, the biography would not be, in some crucial way, "the full story" of the person's life.

The deaths of others merit grief to the extent that those deaths disrupt our autobiographies. This helps shed light on one of the more peculiar emotional features of grief. For many, grief feels like a loss of self, a loss *of* us. "I've lost a part of myself," many grieving people say.[8] Such a remark underscores how grief is often distressing because it is disorienting. The absence of the individual for whom we grieve can permeate our interactions with other people or with objects, thereby rendering day-to-day life strange or alien. Actions or events that previously mattered a great deal come to matter far less; actions or events that mattered hardly at all come to matter far more. Long-established patterns of thought and feeling suddenly seem strange. And because the world suddenly seems foreign, the self can also feel foreign or disjointed. Grief leaves us feeling unfamiliar or unrecognizable to ourselves, almost incorporeal.

Joan Didion, author of the widely read grief memoir *The Year of Magical Thinking*, describes the shock of grief as "obliterative, dislocating to both body and mind," culminating in a confrontation with an "experience of meaninglessness."[9] Lewis called Joy's death "an amputation," sparking a grief that lent his "life a permanently provisional feeling."[10]

That we grieve those in whom we have invested our practical identities helps explain this sense of finding oneself unfamiliar and the world around oneself disorienting. The individuals we grieve for are, in some way, vital to our understandings of who we are and what matters to us. They have been incorporated *into* those understandings and so play crucial roles in our practical identities. When they die then, their deaths represent a threat to a dimension of us. A part of ourselves has (nonliterally) been lost—a practical or ethical part.[11] So when someone in whom we have invested our practical identity dies, our self-conceptions can be shaken, sometimes dramatically (a theme we shall revisit in chapter 3).

6. Grief in All Its Diversity

That we grieve those in whom we have invested our practical identity explains why we grieve the deaths of those with whom we are intimate, those we love, and those to whom we are attached. Those with whom we have intimacy typically will have especially large parts to play in our practical identity. Likewise for those whom we love or to whom we are emotionally attached. Thus, my account of the scope of grief (of the conditions a relationship with another must meet in order for the other's death to intelligibly prompt grief) explains why appealing to intimacy, love, or attachment to mark the limits of grief *seemed* promising.

However, as we have seen, these other three accounts of grief's scope succumb to counterexamples. Yet these counterexamples can be readily handled by my own proposed account.

Take the grief we sometimes experience at the deaths of artists, musicians, political leaders, or other revered or admired public figures. If grieving such public figures requires investing our practical identities in them, the grief we can feel at their deaths is genuine and explicable. In the case of artists and musicians, we often take pleasure in their creative works and performances. Over time, we often form expectations about their works and performances that are incorporated into our implicit conceptions of what is good or valuable for us. Deadheads, Beliebers, or Beatlemaniacs—ardent music fans who eagerly await announcements of upcoming tours or recordings, collect the performers' memorabilia, and plan social gatherings with other fans of their favorite performers—have clearly invested their identities in these artists. How their lives proceed turns on the production of these works and performances. Grief at the deaths of these artists should therefore not surprise us.

In the case of political leaders, identity investment (and therefore grief) can flow from the fact that we often view these individuals as repositories of our personal or collective hopes. The death of Abraham Lincoln, no stranger to grief himself, is a case in point. After his assassination, Lincoln's body was carried more than 1,600 miles by train, stopping in 180 American cities. Thousands of mourners sought the opportunity to view Lincoln's body, many waiting more than five hours to see it pass by in a procession. For African Americans in particular, many of whom saw in Lincoln the chief champion of their liberation, the distress or disbelief was especially acute. As one formerly enslaved person put it, "We have lost our Moses." Some worried that Lincoln's death foretold the restoration of slavery.[12] For those outside the United States, their grief for Lincoln was more clearly tied to their political identities. Lincoln's death resonated in Germany and Italy, nations undergoing challenges similar to those the United States faced concerning national unity; among European anti-slavery groups; and among conservative defenders of the order of law against the forces of rebellion. Those outside the United States who grieved Lincoln thus saw in him and in "the American experiment writ large" an "idealized view of their own aspirations."[13] Here again, the centrality of identity investment plays a clear role in explaining such grief. For those outside the United States who grieved Lincoln, their well-being was not at stake in Lincoln's death nor were they intimate with or attached to him in any significant way. Yet they grieved because his death represented a setback in the pursuit of sociopolitical causes in which their individual practical identities were invested.

Another way in which the grief we feel upon the deaths of particular public figures can rest on having our identities invested in them is when they serve as role models. A budding politician may grieve the death of a well-known leader because she modelled her political tactics or values on that individual. A musician may model his fingering technique or his performance persona on those used by a "guitar hero." In these cases, individuals' conceptions of their professional or vocational identities are intertwined with the public figures whom they emulate.

My account of grief's scope also helps explain how we might grieve for those whom we have come to hate or who disappointed us. Hate and disappointment are not indifference, and we may not be indifferent toward those we have come to hate or who disappointed us precisely because our relationships have the feature—identity investment—that I have suggested must be present for grief to occur. We may hate, or be disappointed in, those whose influence on our self-conception or on our conception of what is good or valuable in life we nevertheless recognize as positive. The soldier from a military family may intensely resent her father for pressuring her into a military career that she nevertheless enjoys and identifies with. A scholar who paid his way through college and graduate study may be disappointed in a parent who could not provide him the education he wanted but nevertheless sees that parent as a source of his central values. Such examples underscore that grief need not rest on relationships that satisfy our hopes. The relationships only need to be the *source* of such hopes.

My account also helps to make sense of grief in short-lived relationships or relationships that "end before they begin," so to speak. The parents of an aborted or miscarried child may nevertheless have had very specific hopes for their lives with that child and have come to see themselves as that child's parent. Likewise, the individual who falls in love with someone at first sight only to have the love object die soon thereafter may have already incorporated the love object into his conception of the future. Grief at such deaths is therefore not surprising despite the fact that such relationships lack the time to develop intimacy or deep familiarity. Similarly, the adopted child who learns of the death of his birth mother may grieve precisely because of a long-standing interest in how the mother may have shaped his personality or values.

Such examples illustrate that grief has as much to do with how things are as with how we would like them to be. Those for whom we grieve are not necessarily those whom we know well or from whom we received particular tangible goods. Grief is instead directed at those who play key roles in how we see ourselves and our lives, those in whom we have invested our hopes and in whom we thereby invested our practical identities. We do grieve for those who shape our lives in causally direct ways, by being our spouses, siblings, co-workers, for example. But we also grieve for those who shape our lives in more indirect and aspirational ways, by serving as the objects of our intentions, the templates for our choices and vocations, or the reservoirs of our ideals.

7. Conclusion

In attempting to make sense of the scope of grief—in trying to identify the conditions a relationship must meet in order for us to grieve—we face a familiar kind of philosophical challenge, namely, how to home in on the essential features of a phenomenon that has a diverse array of manifestations and qualities. The practical identity investment account of these features finds the unity within this diversity, by explaining more paradigmatic cases of grief (grief at the deaths of spouses, family members, and the like) while explaining more atypical cases as well.

A plausible account of grief's scope leaves many crucial questions unanswered. To know for whom we grieve does not yet explain precisely for what we grieve and why. (For comparison: Knowing who you may dance with does not yet explain what dance you perform and why you perform it.) These are the concerns we turn to next.

CHAPTER TWO

What to Expect When You're Grieving

By understanding whom we grieve, we have made it halfway toward meeting this guide's first main objective—to identify the nature of grief. To get the rest of the way, we must grapple with some of the perplexities that grief presents as an emotional phenomenon.

Emotions tend to conform to patterns of cause and effect: Fear, for instance, is the negative feeling caused by our awareness of a threat or risk. Gratitude is the positive feeling caused by our awareness of having been benefitted or fortunate in some way. In concluding that we grieve in response to the deaths of those in whom we have invested our practical identities, we have identified an essential element of grief's emotional pattern: In other words, we have identified grief's proximate cause. But knowing that we grieve in response to the deaths of those with whom we stand in certain kinds of relationships does not yet tell us in what the grief response *consists*. Therefore, we have yet to identify the effects of this cause, or the nature of grief as an emotional condition.

Ascertaining what grief experiences are—beyond what kinds of death causally instigate them—requires addressing several challenges. As we observed in the previous chapter, grief episodes are highly variegated with respect to their sources. We grieve for familiars and for strangers, for those we love and (sometimes) for those we hate, for those who have made our lives better and for those who have made it worse, those with whom we have robust, long-standing relationships and those with whom we have at best fleeting relationships. An adequate account of grief's nature must therefore explain both the *intrapersonal* variability of grief (how a particular person will grieve different deaths differently) and its *interpersonal* variability (how different persons will grieve a particular person's death differently). Can we nevertheless distill an *essence* of grief from this variability? This will be the primary challenge of this chapter.[1]

1. Mood versus Process

The first complication that grief presents is that, unlike most emotional conditions, it seems to consist not in *an* emotion, but in a series of emotions. When invoked expressly in connection with reactions to others' deaths, "grief" is sometimes confined to the feelings of acute sadness elicited by another's death, as in the "throes of grief." The twentieth-century philosopher Ludwig Wittgenstein hints at how such expressions may mislead us into wrongfully *identifying* "grief" with this sadness. Wittgenstein suggests that while uttering "For a second he felt violent pain" is unproblematic, there is something "queer" about the utterance "For a second he felt deep grief." He observes that the queerness of the latter stems from conceptualizing grief as if it were only a "sensation"[2] or an "observation."[3] Grief, Wittgenstein argues, is not like a sensation or observation in being a single state with an easily decipherable beginning and ending in time. Grief instead "describes a pattern which recurs, with different variations in the weave of our life." Grief can thus involve different emotions and is not wholly captured by assimilating it to any one emotion or emotional response: "If a man's bodily expression of sorrow and of joy alternated, say with the ticking of a clock, here we should not have the characteristic formation of the pattern of sorrow or of the pattern of joy."[4] I take Wittgenstein to be stating, in his typically enigmatic way, that grief is something more than an emotional "sensation" or a regular series of such "sensations." Grief has more emotional texture and structure than more basic emotions such as sorrow, joy, anger, or fear. In fact, grief episodes often incorporate many of these emotions.

If Wittgenstein is correct, then one way grief differs from most other emotions is that it lasts longer. This observation invites the possibility that grief is not an emotion but rather a *mood*. Moods, after all, often have longer durations than standard emotions do. A "bad mood" can color an hour, a day, or even a week. Moreover, grief resembles moods in seeming to influence our more specific emotional reactions. To be in, say, a surly mood is (among other things) to react to particular events in ways that are unexpectedly or disproportionately hostile or dismissive. Likewise, grief seems to impact our more specific emotional reactions. A grieving person may take less pleasure in otherwise enjoyable activities, cry at events that would otherwise not elicit tears, "fly off the handle" at others' relatively minor offenses. Grief can thus parallel moods in being a pervasive "meta-emotion," a kind of emotional framework that influences how we react to the world.

Nevertheless, to classify grief as a mood is wrongheaded. For one, moods are often contrasted with emotions by claiming that emotions have, but moods lack, objects.[5] The thought here seems to be that emotions are standardly directed at facts that, in ordinary circumstances, render the emotions explicable or intelligible. When someone becomes angry at an insult, the object of their anger is the insult (or perhaps the individual responsible for it). The anger in question is anger *about* the insult. Moods, on the other hand, have causes but do not seem to have objects. Our moods can be caused by particular facts but are not about those facts. A person's surly mood may be the result of not having eaten lunch, but it is not *about* not having eaten lunch. As we have already seen, grief has a distinct cause, the death of an individual whom we related to in terms of identity investment. But, as will be revealed in this chapter, grief is not "objectless" in this way. Grief, it turns out, does have a particular object that renders it explicable or intelligible.

What grief's object is—what we grieve *about*—will be explained in a later section of this chapter. But there is another set of reasons to resist the claim that grief is a mood. Moods, though they have extended duration and color our emotional responses, act on us in a uniform way. A person in a melancholy mood reacts, with greater frequency or intensity, with sadness to various events; a person in a buoyant mood reacts, with greater frequency or intensity, with glee to various events, and so on. Yet, as Wittgenstein seems to have appreciated, grief can manifest as sadness, but nearly always involves multiple distinct emotional states. Grief is thus less an emotion than an emotional pattern or *process*. This thesis was later popularized by Elisabeth Kübler-Ross[6] and John Bowlby[7] in the "five-stage theory" of grief. Subsequent research has found that the five-stage theory, at least in its canonical five-stage denial-anger-bargaining-depression-acceptance form, is almost certainly incorrect. Many individuals who grieve do not undergo these five particular stages; do not undergo them in this order; or undergo other states as parts of their grief (fear, guilt, etc.).[8] Nevertheless, it has become widely recognized that grief is an emotional process that includes sadness but also other emotional states or reactions. This thesis should not be misunderstood. That grief is a multistage process does not entail sharp temporal boundaries between the emotional stages that constitute a grief episode. A bereaved person might, for instance, simultaneously feel sadness and anger. Similarly, grief episodes can have fuzzy beginnings, particularly in the case of "anticipatory" grief that occurs in the expectation of a person's future death. Grief may also have fuzzy or inconclusive endings, for as many clinical accounts attest, grief-like emotions can recur well after we might expect our grief to have resolved or come to an end.[9] Nor does grief being a multistage process preclude its being (as Wittgenstein remarked) recurrent or cyclical, with particular emotional states occurring repeatedly during a particular grief episode.

2. Finding the One within the Many

That grief is a multistage process sheds light on its intrapersonal and interpersonal variability. Not only will one individual grieve different deaths differently—different individuals will grieve the same death differently. That grief is a process involving multiple emotional states increases the ways in which grief episodes can vary from one another. Some episodes will include depression, others will not; some episodes will include anger, others will not; and so on.

Some may wonder though whether the thesis that grief is an emotional process, whatever its merits in accounting for the *diversity* of grief experiences, flounders in explaining the *unity* of grief episodes. We might, after all, describe an episode of grief not as a single, coherent reaction to the death of a particular other but rather as a series of distinct effects with a common cause. Suppose that Hector reacts to the death of Ivan with a series of emotions: sadness-anger-acceptance. What reason do we have, aside perhaps from convention or convenience, for categorizing these distinct emotions under the umbrella of a single grief episode—Hector grieving Ivan's death—rather than as a sequence of unrelated emotional events? We might equally well describe this as a series of unrelated responses with a common cause (Hector's sadness-at-Ivan's-death, Hector's anger-at-Ivan's-death, Hector's acceptance-of-Ivan's-death) or a series of responses to distinct phenomena (Hector's sadness at losing Ivan, Hector's anger at the injustice of Ivan's dying, Hector's acceptance of Ivan's death). The thesis that grief is a process seems to account for the intrapersonal and interpersonal diversity of grief episodes, but arguably leaves a more fundamental claim, that grief processes are themselves unified emotional episodes, unexplained. And absent some explanation of what unifies the component emotional states of grief into a coherent whole, it may be a mistake to view grief as an emotional process rather than a mere sequence of emotions.

This problem of accounting for the unity of the processes that constitute grief episodes while also acknowledging the diversity of those episodes is formidable. The problem becomes tougher when we take stock of another feature of grief: that it is an activity.

3. Actively Grieving

Emotional experience is often seen as essentially passive. Events around us produce emotions in us, but the control or agency we have with respect to the emotions themselves is mostly indirect. Often we can influence our emotions by influencing what happens to us. (Aware of my tendency to irritation in crowded grocery stores, I can make sure to shop when the store traffic is light.) But our ability to influence what emotions we experience *given* what events occur around us seems much more limited. I may be able to plan my day so I avoid the crowds at the local grocers, but once I am in the crowded store, I am almost certainly going to become irritated. Our choice and actions may not be hostage to the world, but our emotions seem largely hostage to the events that prompt them.

This stereotypical picture of the emotions—as phenomena that assail us, in the face of which we are largely helpless—is definitely overstated. While our emotions cannot be controlled in the sense that we cannot will emotions into and out of existence, our emotions can be managed over time, and it does seem possible to shift our patterns of emotional response and learn healthier, wiser, or more reasonable emotional patterns.

Grief is an example of an emotional condition that is not just a passive state of feeling. Emotions generate behavior. And because grief is a process, it generates behaviors, that is, grief creates a dynamic of feeling and acting as it unfolds. Sadness is common early in grief episodes, for instance. This feeling generates behaviors, many of which involve the public and ritualistic practices of grieving: mourning.[10] A grieving person who attends the deceased's funeral, visits his gravesite, embraces other grieving persons, and so on, demonstrates the behavioral manifestations of sadness. But as grief unfolds, its emotional tenor alters, and so too do the behaviors representative of grief. A person whose grief includes a period of anger may, in a fit of pique, discard some of the deceased loved one's belongings. Later, that same person, her grief having developed into joy or acceptance, might regret having discarded those belongings and may instead spend significant time organizing photos or mementos of the deceased. That "grief" is a noun may lead us to overlook how grief—or perhaps more accurately, *grieving*—is an *activity*, instead of merely a set of passive emotional states. For the process of grief involves an often complex interplay of feeling and action. The bereaved respond to the emotional states of grief with choices and actions. Moreover, these choices and actions can shape grief's subsequent emotional contours. A choice or action motivated by one emotion can sometimes catalyze the bereaved individual's transition to a subsequent "stage" of grief.

In describing grief as an activity, I do not mean that grief is a phenomenon over which we exert *full* control. I merely highlight how grieving is a dynamic process wherein bereaved individuals engage with their emotions and thereby shape both those emotions and the significance they ascribe to those emotions. In this regard, grieving is analogous to musical improvisation. A musician is given a score that provides a template for her activity of performing the piece at hand. But through the improvisations of varying tempo, key, etc., she in effect "composes" a new piece whose parameters were originally established by the score. In like manner, grieving is a process wherein individuals engage with an emotional sequence not entirely of their own choosing but which they can imbue with significance that transcends the emotions that serve as the affective ingredients of grief episodes.

So, although we do not orchestrate grief, we do not stand in a wholly passive, spectator-like relationship to it either. Grief is something we do, rather than something that happens to us.

Unfortunately, though, this second distinguishing feature of grief—that the process of grief is an activity encompassing both feeling and action—does not ameliorate the problem of understanding how grief episodes possess the unity required to categorize them as coherent emotional experiences rather than sequences of discrete emotional states. In fact, that grief is an activity arguably exacerbates it.

Notice that grief can only be *an* activity if grief episodes have an underlying emotional unity. And on what basis can we claim that the various choices or actions that ensue when individuals undergo the affective states that comprise grief contribute to a single activity? We engage in many activities that have various choices and actions among their components. In these cases, the choices and actions derive their intelligibility or significance from the larger activity and its point or purpose. Again, to engage in musical improvisation is to make many on-the-spot choices about when to vary tempo, change key, and so on. But these choices, and the actions they give rise to, are nevertheless conceptually and practically linked by the fact that they are elements of performing a given piece. So too for many other complex human activities. To pay your bills, you often need to engage in a number of component choices or actions: gathering the bills, prioritizing the order of their payment, ensuring payment, tabulating the deductions from your account. In such cases, an individual's choices or actions count as part of the same activity, despite the heterogeneity of the choices or actions themselves, thanks to how those choices and actions contribute singly to the activity's point or purpose. This is why, when we ask those engaged in these activities what they are doing, two answers— one fine-grained, one coarse-grained—seem equally appropriate. If in the midst of paying your bills, you are asked "what are you doing?" a fine-grained response ("entering bill payment dates with the bank") is apt, but so too is a more coarse-grained response ("paying the bills"), for you are doing the latter *by way of* the former.

It is less clear in the case of the activity of grief, however, that two such answers are equally available to the bereaved individual.

A bereaved individual planning a memorial service can certainly offer the fine-grained answer, "I'm planning the memorial service." And of course, she could equally well offer the coarse-grained answer, "I'm grieving." But even if she herself grasps how her planning the memorial service also counts as her grieving, how this relation is possible is not obvious. How can crying, visiting the deceased's favorite restaurant, and planning a memorial service constitute ways of engaging *in one and the same activity*, to wit, grieving?

What we are doing in the activity of grieving is thus more elusive than what we are doing in many other complex human activities. And skeptics might assert that this is evidence that there is no such activity of grieving—only a set of choices and actions that do not coalesce around any larger point or purpose, a set with a common causal origin but with no holistic character to render it a unified endeavor. Why should we not say, then, that grieving individuals undergo emotions that both shape and are shaped by choice and actions, but these choices and actions are metaphysically discrete, bearing no intrinsic relationship to one another (or to those emotions)?

That the process of grief is an activity, punctuated both by emotional states and by choice or action, thus makes the unity of grief episodes more rather than less obscure.

4. Paying Attention

So far, we have focused on two crucial elements of grief: its causes (that is, whose deaths prompt it) and its dynamics (an active, emotionally laden process). The unity of grief begins to come into view when we notice the interplay between grief's causes and its dynamics.

Our emotions can provide us evidence regarding the significance of the events that cause them. Emotions standardly do this in a direct and unambiguous way: The fear we experience in response to the smell of smoke warns of fire, a threat to our lives or well-being. An insult generates anger, an indicator that our pride has been wounded.

Grief, in contrast, divulges the significance of another's death in a more haphazard or cryptic way. Certain elements of grief—sadness, notably—seem to behave as standard emotions do: A grieving person undergoing sadness "learns" (if it were not already apparent) that the absence of the deceased is a cause for dismay or distress. But other emotional elements of grief do not wear their significance on their sleeves. What do the fear, joy, anger, or anxiety that some experience during grief episodes signify about the deceased or our relationships to them? And what does the totality of the emotions that comprise a grief episode signify? Grief, many have observed, is a more coy emotional state, a "questioning" emotion that reveals its significance haltingly and piecemeal.

Our engagement with our own grief is, as we noted above, active rather than passive: If grief is to be informative about the significance of another's death, it will do so thanks to its serving as a species of *attention*. As the philosopher of emotions Michael Brady has argued, emotions sometimes do not immediately settle the significance of the events that prompt them. Rather, they instead motivate us to attend to the events that prompt them, interrogating the significance of those events to us. Such emotions, Brady argues, do not terminate possible inquiry into the significance of the events that cause them. They instead instigate and sustain it.[11] Grief, I propose, is a paradigm case of emotionally catalyzed attention. For attention is not best thought of as a single mental activity or state.[12] Attention is instead an ongoing endeavor that includes exercises of our constituent mental powers (perception, emotion, intention, etc.).

To attend to some fact or phenomenon is to prioritize it in consciousness, thereby consigning other phenomena to the periphery of one's mental life. Grief, we have noted, has a similar structural character. We are brought to grief by the death of another, and grief's ending is marked by a diminution in attention to the deceased other. While grief contains elements that are largely passive or outside our influence (the affective states of sadness, etc.), it persists over time and is in some measure an agential process we can guide or control in an improvisational manner. Grief thus "crosscuts the usual division of the mind," engaging "the cognitive and the conative, the perceptual and the intellectual, the active and the passive, the epistemic and the practical."[13] That grief is a form of attention does not entail that this attention is equally gripping or galvanizing in every grief episode. But even in less intense or long-lasting grief episodes, the deceased individual occupies an abnormal proportion of the bereaved individual's awareness.

5. What We Grieve For

That grief is a process of active attention identifies the structural features of grief. But we still lack a crucial ingredient to understand the nature of grief. The previous chapter identified the *material* object of grief. The material object of some attitude—or in the case of grief, the material object of the various attitudes and mental acts that constitute a grief process or episode—is the particular fact or state of affairs that makes it such that an individual has the attitude. When smelling smoke leads to fear, the smoke (or, more accurately, the fire it portends) is the material object of the fear. With respect to grief, its material object is the death of a particular individual in whom the bereaved has invested their practical identity. To know the material object of some attitude is to know the fact that explains its occurrence. But the material object of an attitude does not necessarily inform us of an attitude's *formal* object.[14] An attitude's formal object corresponds to the true description of its material object such that it is logically intelligible for the attitude to be directed at that material object. What is it, again, about the smell of smoke that renders it intelligible or defensible to be afraid? Note that there are innumerable truths about smoke that do not help answer that question: that smoke results from consumption of oxygen, that smoke caused by burning rubber has a different odor from wood smoke, that smoke can be a particularly difficult smell to erase from clothing and furniture. None of these facts about smoke help to *justify* our fear of what it portends. Rather, what renders our fear defensible or intelligible is the fact that the smoke signals the presence of an unexpected threat. It is therefore the threat posed that serves as the formal object of the fear induced by smelling smoke.

Let us now entertain the parallel question about grief's formal object: What fact about grief's material object—the deaths of those who matter to us—explains why we *should* feel grief in response to that fact? Put in terms of attention, we now know what facts prompt us to pay attention to the fact that someone in whom we have invested our practical identity has died. But we do not yet know what it is about those facts that renders attention to those facts intelligible or defensible. How does grief come to grip us as it does?

6. Object Is Loss of Well-Being to Deceased?

Assume that the various emotional stages that constitute grief— anger, sadness, joy, for instance—are all ways of attending to some fact or other. To this point, we have spoken of this fact generically, and perhaps tritely, as a "loss." But there are several candidates for the exact loss that serves as grief's formal object.

One candidate for the loss that serves as grief's formal object is the acute sorrow for what the *deceased* have lost by dying. When deaths are premature or unexpected, part of our grief responds to the belief that the dead were deprived or ill-treated by death—that had they lived longer, they would have enjoyed various goods that would have made their lives better as a whole.[15] And because we stand in the right sort of relationship with the deceased—one of identity investment—in which we are likely to empathize with them, it seems to follow that the loss that constitutes the formal object of grief is the loss that the deceased suffered. Despite the loss being, strictly speaking, suffered by the deceased, our empathy with them is likely to make that loss one that we suffer as well, if only vicariously.

However, the losses suffered by the deceased cannot actually be the object of our grief. First and foremost, we grieve for those whose deaths do *not* represent losses of well-being to them. The parents of Nancy Cruzan, who lived in a coma for eight years, appeared to grieve her death, even though it is difficult to imagine that, given her condition, she had much to lose by dying. Additionally, grief is intelligible even when a person's death is beneficial to them. Relatives and friends of those who opt for assisted dying appear to grieve such deaths, even though they may support their loved ones' choice to die and wholeheartedly believe death is beneficial to them. Thus, there are genuine cases of grief for which the description "the deceased suffered a loss by dying" does not apply. And yet grieving such deaths does not seem misplaced or irrational in these instances.[16]

Another way to appreciate why death's badness for the deceased cannot be the formal object of grief is that it has perverse implications for how grief could be reduced. If death's badness for the deceased were the formal object of grief, then grief would be reduced if death were less bad for the deceased. And this, in turn, could be accomplished by making the life the deceased would have had if she had lived longer worse than she had anticipated. But this seems like a farcical strategy for lessening the sufferings of grief. Suppose Jimmy is grieving the death of his sister Keshia. Their brother Lonnie (perhaps believing that the formal object of grief is what the deceased lost by dying) comes up with a plan to help Jimmy with his grief: He spreads nasty rumors about Keshia among her friends and ruins her collection of vintage vinyl. Lonnie reasons that this way, Jimmy has less to grieve for because Keshia's death is now less bad for her than Jimmy realizes. Keshia, after all, manages to avoid these misfortunes by dying when she did.[17] Now ask: Would Jimmy have less reason to grieve Keshia's death than he did before? Would his grief diminish in response to Lonnie's actions? Would Jimmy have reason to thank Lonnie for helping him manage his grief? The answer to all three questions (surely) is "no." This illustrates that the intensity or amount of grief we ought to feel does not track with how bad death is for the deceased.[18] If so, then this makes it even less likely that what we grieve for is the badness of death for the deceased whose death caused our grief in the first place.

The losses suffered by the deceased due to death therefore cannot be the formal object of grief, and these losses are not the basic fact that is the ongoing focus of grief's attention.

7. Object Is Loss of Well-Being to Bereaved?

A second candidate for grief's formal object is the loss suffered by the bereaved because of the death of the deceased. As Martha Nussbaum emphasizes, we grieve those on whom we rely as contributors to our flourishing.[19] This is a more promising candidate than the losses suffered by the deceased because it locates grief more egocentrically: in the concerns or well-being of the grieving person.

But this hypothesis also falls short of the mark because there are intelligible instances of grief for which the bereaved has suffered no loss in well-being due to the death of the individual in question. For instance, there will be instances of grief in which the bereaved may have suffered some loss in well-being, but this loss is smaller than the gains in well-being that result from the very same death. A care provider for someone with a fatal illness may suffer a loss in well-being upon the latter's death (say, because he lost a conversational partner) but may nevertheless enjoy an overall increase in well-being as a consequence (because providing such care is exhausting and time-consuming). Even so, grief on the caregiver's part would not be untoward. In some instances, grief occurs in the absence of any apparent loss of well-being for the bereaved. As we noted in chapter 1, while we grieve those in whom we invest our practical identities, that is nevertheless compatible with those same individuals not increasing, or even detracting from, our actual well-being. Children grieve the deaths of abusive or neglectful parents, and divorced individuals grieve the deaths of spouses from whom they have long been estranged. The relationship between grief and losses of well-being for the bereaved is thus more contingent than is commonly supposed. Not everyone for whom we grieve makes, has made, or will make a positive contribution to our well-being.

Grief's formal object being the loss of well-being suffered by the bereaved is also incompatible with the sense that what the bereaved have lost is irreplaceable.[20] Many of those we grieve provide us various goods. But our grief is not directed at some bundle of goods. If grief's formal object were the goods provided by the deceased while alive, then it ought to diminish once we find other sources of those goods. But it is unlikely that grief does, or ought to, abate once the bereaved identify new sources of the goods that the deceased previously provided. Seneca's infamous analogy between a deceased friend and a stolen tunic is cringeworthy precisely because it misses how grief is directed at something more than that set of goods the deceased provided to the bereaved. We might agree with Seneca that "a man who has lost his one and only tunic through robbery" who then "chooses to bewail his plight rather than look about him for some way to escape the cold" is indeed an "utter fool."[21] Yet we also think, contra Seneca, that someone who lost his one and only wife, business partner, or eldest child *is* a fool for trying to "replace" these individuals by ticking off a laundry list of goods that those individuals had once provided him. And as we noted in chapter 1, attachment (which is common in our relationships with those whose deaths we grieve) does not seem reducible to the goods that those to whom we are attached provide us, i.e., attachment hinges as much on how these goods are provided as on the goods themselves.

Thus, neither the loss of well-being suffered by the deceased nor the parallel loss suffered by the bereaved is the formal object of grief. It is possible for the activity of grief—the ongoing process of emotional attention—to occur even when neither type of loss has been incurred.

8. Grief's Object Is the Loss of the Pre-Mortem Relationship with the Deceased

Before turning to the best candidate for grief's formal object, let us review the progress we have made so far in identifying the nature of grief.

An adequate account of grief's nature must identify the essential features of grief capable of accounting for the intrapersonal and interpersonal diversity of grief experiences, as well as accounting for the unity of grief experiences, i.e., how the various elements of grief episodes cohere together to constitute a single grief experience. We concluded that grief is an active process of emotional attention, incorporating both feeling and choice, causally instigated by the death of someone in whom the bereaved has invested her identity. The object of grief seems to be some sort of "loss." However, neither losses in well-being suffered by the deceased nor by the bereaved are essential to grief. We are therefore seeking an account of the loss incurred by the bereaved that is essential to grief, a loss some true description of which provides the formal object needed to render grief intelligible.

The preceding discussion of Seneca's analogy between a friend's death and the theft of one's cloak suggests a way forward with respect to grief's formal object. Grief, we concluded earlier, is not fundamentally concerned with the goods whose deprivation we suffer due to a person's death. Grief responds instead to the loss of the *person*. But even this does not pinpoint grief's formal object. For as we saw in chapter 1, grief's disorientation often manifests as a species of emotional phantom limb, in which an aspect of oneself has seemingly gone missing, resulting in feelings of alienation, self-consciousness, or uncanniness as one goes about one's day-to-day life. Grief thus seems to estrange us from familiar patterns previously defined by one's relationship with the deceased. Essential to grief, I propose, is that *one's relationship with the deceased cannot continue in precisely the same guise it had when the deceased was still alive.* The death of an individual in whom one's identity is invested necessitates a transformation in one's relationship to that individual. This transformation can take many forms: Conversations, rituals, and activities involving the deceased no longer occur. Some conflicts between the bereaved and the deceased can no longer be brought to light or adjudicated. Other conflicts are such that death seems to bring them out into the open. We no longer harbor hopes for what the deceased might do or become. The bereaved can forgive the deceased, but not vice versa. We cannot plan with or around the deceased as we once did. And of course we may lose many tangible goods due to their deaths: income, housing, economic security, emotional support and security, inspiration and insight.

In short, the deaths of those for whom we grieve alter the trajectory of our relationships with the deceased in at least some way. Their deaths foreclose some possibilities for our relationships with them, while opening up others. And because those for whom we grieve are those around whom we have constructed our expectations for how we hope our lives will go, we grieve for the relationships that their deaths transform. The deaths of others shift our possible ways of relating to them, and so our relationship with the deceased ought to change accordingly. Note that only rarely will this transformation consist in an outright *destruction* of that relationship. In fact, grieving is possible so long as the bereaved holds the deceased in memory. And in most cases, the transformation falls short of the relationship ceasing altogether.[22] So, tempting as it is to describe these phenomena in terms of the bereaved's loss *of the deceased*, it is more accurately described as the bereaved's losing *their prior relationship with the deceased*. As one pair of grief researchers put it:

the empirical reality is that people *do not* relinquish their ties to the deceased, withdraw their cathexes,[23] or "let them go." What occurs for survivors is a transformation from what had been a relationship operating on several levels of actual, symbolic, internalized, and imaging relatedness to one in which the actual ("living and breathing") relationship has been lost, but the other forms remain or may even develop in more elaborate forms.[24]

C. S. Lewis nicely captured this by comparing marital relationships to a dance or the change of seasons. Grief, he wrote,

> follows marriage as normally as marriage follows courtship or autumn follows summer. It is not a truncation of the process but one of its phases; not the interruption of the dance but the next figure.[25]

Because the relationships in question are identity-constituting, the death can produce a relationship crisis for the bereaved. The "questioning" involved in grief often revolves around figuring out how to proceed forward with life given that a significant person—a person whose existence had made one's life make sense at some level—has died. But in questioning how we will live without the other, we are obliquely questioning ourselves: Who are we to become, now that a central facet of who we were is no longer so?

That grief's formal object—that for which we grieve and that captures our attention in grief—is the relationship with the deceased that the latter's death necessarily transforms, where this also includes hopes or expectations of how it might have been, satisfies the criteria we have identified for an adequate account of grief's nature.

First, that the bereaved's relationship with the deceased has been transformed or disrupted by the latter's death is a strong candidate for the essence of grief due to its ubiquity in the grief experience. The deaths of those in whom our practical identities are invested should naturally lead to heightened emotional attention to that fact, even if (for example) neither the deceased nor the bereaved suffered any loss in well-being as a result of the former's death. Note that the relationship transformation wrought by another's death need not be extensive, comprehensive, or traumatic in order to elicit grief. As shall be explored in greater detail in chapters 3 and 4, the relationship "crisis" engendered by another's death is simultaneously a crisis in practical identity, that description under which we value ourselves and take ourselves to have reasons to act as we do. We suffer in grief in part because another's death forces us to reconfigure our practical identities. In the case of grief, the threat is ethical instead of literal or physical.[26] But these "crises" can be mild and may only involve very modest reworkings of our practical identities. For example, we should expect that a doctor will grieve the death of a long-time patient differently than they would that same patient's spouse, sibling, or professional colleague. But in each case, the bereaved individual will be compelled to modify her relationship with the deceased, even if only in subtle and easily navigable ways. Grief varies in its intensity, tenor, and duration precisely because relationships vary in their intensity, tenor, and duration.

But these variations—the intrapersonal and interpersonal diversity of grief episodes—are readily decipherable if, as I have argued, grief's formal object is the transformation of the bereaved's relationship with the deceased. The relationships between pairs of deceased individuals and those who grieve them vary along multiple dimensions. Hence there are as many possibilities for how a person's death may transform the relationship she had with a surviving person, and hence as many possibilities for grief, as there are different sorts of relationships. One and the same individual will therefore not grieve different deaths in just the same way, nor will different individuals grieve one and the same death in just the same way.

This leaves a final feature that an adequate account of grief's nature must explain: the unity of grief episodes, that is, how the various affective states and choices that constitute a grief episode are to be understood as a unified response instead of a sequence of unrelated responses with a common causal origin in the death of another. Because grief attends to the relationship transformed by another's death, grief episodes will likely include states and choices that reflect the sometimes complex relationships we bear to one another. Consider a relatively standard case of grief: An adult grieves the death of an aged parent. Children's relationships with their parents often have strikingly intricate emotional dynamics. Part of the reason for this is that both parties to the relationship undergo dramatic personal changes throughout the relationship's course. Children are born vulnerable and dependent on their parents. Later in life, struggles between parents and children over the latter's independence and autonomy are common. The roles of parents and children overlap at a later stage in life, as the children themselves become adults with professional lives and perhaps children of their own, children with whom they may try to replicate or reject their relationships with their own parents. This stage, in which parents and their adult children are effectively peers, can give way to a stage in which the early stage of the relationship is reversed such that parents become materially and emotionally dependent on their adult children. Each of these chapters or stages of the child-parent relationship will be characterized by particular emotional patterns. Given the panoply of emotions found in the history of such a relationship, it would hardly be surprising if the parent's death—which, I have argued, triggers in the adult child a focus on how this event must necessarily transform her relationship with that parent—generates an equally diverse emotional response. As we grieve, our emotional states shift, directed at different aspects of the relationship we had (or hoped to have had) with the deceased. In the case of a grief episode prompted by a parent's death, there is hardly an emotion we could not envision arising: the usual candidates such as sadness, but also gratitude, resentment, confusion, fear, regret, nostalgia, guilt, joy, etc. This need not mean a one-to-one correspondence between the stages that constitute a grief episode and the stages of a child's relationship to a parent. But grief episodes will tend to recapitulate, at least in part, the emotions found within the bereaved's relationship to the deceased. This in turn validates the expectation that relationships with greater levels of intimacy or identification between the bereaved and the deceased are likely to lead to grief episodes with greater levels of emotional complexity.

That grief's formal object is the transformation of the bereaved's relationship with the deceased thus explains how the diversity of actions and choices in a grief episode constitute a coherent whole: The particular affective states that constitute a grief episode are directed at different aspects of the grieving person's relationship with the deceased and are collectively directed at the transformation in one's relationship with the deceased that death necessitates. The questioning that often permeates grief can thus be seen as the bereaved individual's attempt to, first, connect her grief-related emotions and choices to the deceased and her relationship with the deceased, and second, to connect the various grief-related emotions and choices together in order to arrive at a holistic grasp of her relationship to the deceased and how she might best maintain that relationship.

A final point regarding grief's formal object: I argued earlier that losses in well-being for either the deceased or the bereaved are not essential to grief. That the formal object of grief is the bereaved's relationship to the deceased transformed by the latter's death helps us see why such losses are nevertheless initially plausible candidates for grief's formal object. Many grief episodes will be rooted in relationships in which the well-being of the bereaved, of the deceased, or both are at stake. Hence, the death of the latter will understandably generate emotional responses focused on well-being and the particular goods that the bereaved or the deceased may have lost due to the latter's death. Much of the bereaved's grief activity will therefore attend to these losses and amount to an attempt to identify, quantify, articulate, and perhaps counteract them. But again, grief is possible even in the absence of losses of, or threats to, the well-being of the parties involved.

9. Grieving for Those Who Survive Death

There is one final consideration that, in my estimation, speaks strongly in favor of my view about grief's formal object.

To this point, we have analyzed grief without regard to grieving individuals' beliefs about death or mortality. But as we know, many people, especially but not exclusively religious believers, believe that death is not the cessation of a person's existence. Rather, death is a metaphysical transition. The deceased cease to exist in their normal earthly condition but continue to exist posthumously. Among those with such a worldview, opinions differ about what that posthumous condition is and what facts determine what that condition is like: Some believe in salvation or damnation, others in the continuation in some other embodied condition such as reincarnation, some in the continuation of an immaterial soul, others in the resurrection of one's body. But all such believers deny that death as we ordinarily understand it is the end of a person's existence. There is, in short, an afterlife.

Believers in the afterlife grieve in response to the deaths of those in whom they have invested their practical identities. Clearly, such believers cannot be grieving merely the fact that the deceased do not exist. For in their eyes, the deceased *do* exist. But their grief is difficult to understand if we adopt any other view of grief's object besides my own.

If grief's object were the loss of well-being for the deceased, this might explain *some* instances of grief among believers in an afterlife. For instance, if one believed that the deceased, due to her impiety or immorality, was fated to eternal torment, then perhaps the believer grieves for the suffering the deceased would be facing. But of course not every bereaved believer in the afterlife believes that the person for whom they grieve is destined for hell. The death of Pope John Paul II elicited widespread grief among Catholics, who believed (presumably) that the pontiff was saved rather than damned. And even for less well-known figures, believers in the afterlife grieve them ("he/she/they are looking down on us from heaven") despite their high levels of confidence that the deceased is undergoing ecstasy rather than torment. Indeed, among Christians and non-Christians alike, belief in hell is declining, especially when compared to the more resilient belief in heaven.[27] A large number of those who believe in the afterlife must therefore believe it is impossible for those whose deaths they grieve to be harmed by death. Granted, it could be that the deceased lose out on some earthly goods upon their death. The deceased might have had a happier or more meaningful life had they lived longer. But if the afterlife conjecture is true, in many cases, the eternal bliss of heaven will greatly exceed those earthly losses. Thus, the fact that believers in the afterlife genuinely grieve is difficult to reconcile with the notion that they grieve for what the deceased have lost by dying.

Hence, believers in the afterlife must be grieving some loss to themselves. What loss? Notice that the loss cannot be the termination of the relationship with the deceased. After all, not only have the deceased continue to exist, they may continue to relate to the bereaved, and vice versa. Bereaved individuals often attempt to communicate with the deceased as if they were alive—in the case of believers in the afterlife, that communication is not merely symbolic. They understand themselves as literally being able to interact with the deceased. Conversely, many believers in the afterlife also contend that the deceased communicate with them, through voices, visions, symbols, among other modes. Their relationship persists, albeit on different terms and with a different trajectory than it had when the deceased person was alive.

We are left, then, with the view of grief's object that I favor: that bereaved individuals who believe in an afterlife grieve the loss of their relationship with the deceased as it was. Their relationships survive in the form of "continuing bonds" with the deceased.[28] This is the only hypothesis consistent with the fact that believers in the afterlife grieve and with the implications their beliefs systems have on how they grieve.

10. Conclusion

Grief thus seems to scramble the familiar categories philosophers have relied upon to analyze our emotions. It resembles standard emotions in having both a material and formal object, but differs from standard emotions in generating active attention toward its object and that object's evaluative significance. In persisting over time and coloring our emotional temperament, grief resembles moods, but it differs from moods, first in having a discernible object, namely, the loss of the relationship as it was with someone in whom our practical identities are invested, and second, in having multiple emotional states that contribute to it. Viewing grief as a process of active emotional attention toward the transformation of a relationship caused by the death of the other member of that relationship does justice to the diversity of individuals for whom we grieve and the diversity of ways in which we grieve them.

Equipped with this richer understanding of the nature of grief, we can now turn toward several crucial ethical questions concerning grief.

- How can it be beneficial or desirable to engage in the activity of grieving, that is, of attending to the relationship another's death has transformed, especially in light of the fact that grief nearly always involves painful or arduous emotions? Why, if at all, should we be glad for the opportunity to grieve? What *good* is there in grief?
- In what sense can grief be a *rational* response to the events that prompt it?
- How, if at all, can we make sense of grief as a moral imperative? How could there possibly be a *duty* to grieve?

Let us now put our account of grief's nature to use in investigating these questions.

CHAPTER THREE

Finding Ourselves
in Grief

Jack Lewis underwent an arduous grief episode. Perhaps it illustrates, albeit in a different way from that advanced by ancient philosophers, why grief should be avoided, even feared: Grief can be psychologically taxing, even tortuous. To read about Lewis's grief is a harrowing experience. Joy's death induced in him a state not only of profound suffering but of upheaval. Whatever good may have come of his ordeal, it cannot compete with the acute suffering he experienced. Lewis's grief episode is almost enough to wish that we could be spared grief altogether.

At the same time though, even if Lewis might have benefitted from grieving *less*, it is hard to shake the sense that it would not have been beneficial for him to grieve *not at all*. The absence of grief would seem to solve Lewis's problem, admittedly. But perhaps it would do so only to deprive him of an experience that seems worthwhile and especially human. To use a medical analogy, perhaps his not grieving would eliminate his "symptoms" without addressing the underlying illness. Even if grief is sometimes profoundly difficult, would we really be better off without it?

To test this hypothesis, we turn to a novel-cum-thought-experiment about grief by another prominent twentieth-century thinker.

Albert Camus's *The Stranger* is probably the best-known literary depiction of existential alienation. For the novel's protagonist, Meursault, neither his work nor his personal relationships have any emotional resonance. Aside from longings for sex and revenge, Meursault reacts to the world around him with blasé disinterest. He is an indifferent man in a seemingly indifferent world. It is no coincidence, then, that Camus used grief (or the lack thereof) to book-end his tale of Meursault.

As the novel begins, Meursault prepares to travel to the funeral of his "Maman." Although Meursault's primary reaction to his mother's death is a preoccupation with the logistics of attending the funeral, readers are nevertheless primed to expect that he will grieve in more or less conventional ways. For before his departure, Meursault appears to self-consciously occupy what Elisabeth Kübler-Ross would later hypothesize[1] is the first stage of grief, namely, denial: "For the present, it's almost as if Mother weren't really dead. The funeral will bring it home to me, put an official seal on it, so to speak."[2] However, Meursault's subsequent "grief" is so inauthentic that he can hardly be said to grieve at all. Though quite aware of the conventions associated with mourning, he refuses to view his mother's body and spends his time during the funeral distracted by minute details of his surroundings and fellow mourners. The expected focus of Meursault's grief, his mother, hardly appears in his consciousness at all. He participates in conventional rituals of mourning without actually grieving.

Later, at his trial, Meursault's prosecutors introduce no evidence at all regarding the factual circumstances concerning the murder of which he is accused. They instead call character witnesses who testify to the deficiency of Meursault's grief. According to these witnesses, Meursault responded to his mother's death by going on a hedonistic bender. Having neither "shed a single tear" for Maman nor lingered at her grave, he had a cigarette and a café au lait before proceeding to enjoy "shameless orgies" the very next day. Meursault's lawyer finally divines this prosecutorial strategy and objects:

> "Is my client on trial for having buried his mother, or for killing a man?" he asked.
>
> There were some titters in court. But then the Prosecutor sprang to his feet and, draping his gown round him, said he was amazed at his friend's ingenuousness in failing to see that between these two elements of the case there was a vital link. They hung together psychologically, if he might put it so. "In short," he concluded, speaking with great vehemence, "I accuse the prisoner of behaving at his mother's funeral in a way that showed he was already a criminal at heart."[3]

Ultimately, Meursault is convicted not for killing an Arab on a beach, but for failing to grieve.

The Stranger is certainly not a conventional grief memoir. Meursault undertakes none of the self-probing and undergoes none of the emotional torment we find in Lewis's A Grief Observed, for instance. Meursault's disinclination (or perhaps inability) to grieve reflects a profound alienation or detachment from others and from the world. For him, grief can only be (as Camus himself would later explain) a "game" that he happens to refuse to play.[4]

The Stranger is of course a work of fiction, not intended to be a guide to living. We are presumably not meant to treat Meursault as a role model. But the agonies of grief, so vividly depicted by Lewis, may persuade us that we should at least wish to be like

Meursault, inoculated against grief by our detachment from others. The case for wishing to be rid of grief is strong: Researchers have concluded that among major life stressors, grief at the deaths of those close to us (our parents or spouses, for instance) ranks near the top, exceeding the stresses of unemployment, divorce, or incarceration.[5] Grief can also take on the cast of an illness, as bereaved individuals manifest physical "symptoms" of grief such as sleeplessness, digestive difficulties, tremors, and shortness of breath. And occasionally, grief plays a role in killing us.[6] Why not therefore see Meursault's inability to grieve as the unexpected upside of his alienated state of being?

Experiences such as Lewis's illustrate that we humans have good reasons to be ambivalent about grief. And perhaps Lewis's own grief was ultimately bad for him.[7] While we lament the magnitude of Jack Lewis's grief, to infer that we would be better off free of grief—that with respect to grief, Meursault has it better than Lewis—is hasty. Again, we might wish that Lewis's grief had been *less* traumatic. And to call grief a game, a frivolity with no greater significance outside itself, trivializes that experience. If Meursault's lack of grief betrays his lack of humanity, our grief seems to reveal ours. Although painful, grief is also essential and, in some elusive way, *good*. One test of this intuition: What would those who cared for Lewis *for his sake* prefer, that he undergo the emotionally fraught experience of grieving Joy or that he react as Meursault did to the death of *maman*, blithely and without any sign of significant grief at all?[8] I would venture the former. Even very painful grief episodes have something to recommend them to the bereaved. The Meursaults of the world are therefore not better off for avoiding grief, and if they believe otherwise, so much the worse for them.

We arrive at essentially the same conclusion if we ponder how we should respond to the sufferings others undergo in the course of grief. Ordinarily, that another person is undergoing suffering provides us a moral reason to relieve that suffering. Yet the duty to eliminate suffering, Troy Jollimore observes, does not seem to apply to the sufferings of grief. Supporting the bereaved can ameliorate their situation or make it more manageable. But it does not follow that it would be morally unobjectionable to attempt to dispel their grief altogether. If one had a pill that would "wipe out" the grief of a bereaved friend, it would seem wrong to offer it to the friend.[9] That the sufferings of grief fall outside our duty to relieve suffering hints that grief is in some way of value to the bereaved.

That grief is (at least can be) good for us is nevertheless difficult to square with how grief *feels*—its phenomenology, as philosophers would say. Some measure of mental pain is inherent to grieving. As we noted in chapter 2, grief generally involves other emotional states besides pain, such as anger, guilt, confusion, and disorientation, many of which are also affectively bad, that is, they are states we do not enjoy being in and will often take active measures to avoid. The emotional preponderance of grief therefore feels bad. Lewis, let's recall, is haunted by his grief—not merely sad, but shaken and lost. His grief episode illustrates how grief is often troubling, sometimes terrible. What then can be said in defense of the intuition that his grief was a *benefit* to him nevertheless?

What I call the *paradox of grief* is the confluence of these observations:

- Grief feels bad, and so should be avoided or lamented.
- Grief is valuable such that we (and others) ought not avoid it altogether and should be grateful that we grieve.

In suggesting that grief is valuable, I have in mind the value that grief has for or to the bereaved—how my grief could be good for me, your grief good for you, Lewis's grief good for Lewis, etc. This is not to deny that grief could be good in other ways. Grieving with others in acts or rituals of mourning could be good for other people, by (for example) providing them comfort or enriching our relationships with them. In this sense, grief could give rise to various *moral* goods.[10] But in keeping with the egocentric nature of grief—how it responds to the transformation of the bereaved individual's relationship with the deceased—the paradox of grief concerns the thought that grief feels bad *for* the bereaved but could nevertheless be beneficial *to* her. This chapter offers a partial resolution of this paradox; the subsequent chapter completes my attempt to resolve this paradox.

That the paradox of grief is genuine can be seen by observing that there is no correlative paradox for other comparably stressful life events. There is unlikely to be a paradox of imprisonment, for example. Some good can arise from being imprisoned, but it is unlikely that we would recommend or prefer imprisonment for those we care about for their own sake. Nor is there likely to be a paradox of unemployment. Again, unemployment can benefit a person in some ways, but it is unlikely to be a condition we would recommend or prefer for those we care about for their own sake. Moreover, we would not suppose that a human life in which a person was never imprisoned or unemployed was a life badly lived, a life somehow less than full or complete. Grief, in contrast, often contributes to a well-lived human life. Grief therefore has *something* to recommend it. Were that not so, "a person who did not grieve would be considered fortunate, like an athlete who has a high threshold of pain, or a risk taker who remains unafraid in circumstances that would scare the wits out of most normal people."[11] But immunity from grief is presumably not a stroke of good fortune.

The question at hand is what is it that recommends grief— what, in other words, is good about grief? An adequate resolution of the paradox of grief seems to require identifying such a good and then showing that this good enables grief to at least *sometimes* be beneficial to those who grieve. Note this "sometimes": We should not expect every grief episode to prove beneficial to the person who grieves. It will sometimes be true that the pain and other negative emotions in a grief episode are so persistent or intense that, whatever goods that episode may provide, they cannot measure up in magnitude to the bad-making features of that episode. Resolving the paradox of grief does not require that every grief episode benefit the bereaved. It requires only that we show that grief *can* be good for us and that good grief is realistically attainable for us. A satisfactory resolution of the paradox only necessitates showing how grief is *paradigmatically* good.

In seeking a good that can resolve this paradox, we need not identify some good that is *unique* to grief. It may well be that whatever value grief has is shared by other activities. Nevertheless, I hope to identify a good that is at least *distinctive* to grief. The good in question should be distinctive to grief in that grief is an especially fruitful way to attain that good—that, of the various ways we might realize this good, grief is particularly well-suited for us to realize it. Indeed, grief should be sufficiently well-suited to realizing that good that no other activity is likely to be equally well-suited to it; grief should, with respect to whatever good(s) it affords us, be effectively irreplaceable as a tool for realizing that good.

1. The Activity of Grief and Its Purpose

In order to home in on what is good about grief, we must remind ourselves of some key claims from prior chapters. We established in chapter 1 that we grieve for those in whom we are eudaimonically invested, those whose existence is incorporated into our practical identities and who we see as fundamental to our projects, commitments, and concerns. And we established in chapter 2 that grief is a multistage process, an emotionally laden activity in which a bereaved individual attends to the loss of her relationship with the deceased, where the "loss" need not mean (and typically will not mean) that the relationship with the deceased ends. Rather, the grieving "survivor" grieves because her relationship with the deceased must change in light of the latter's death. As we observed in chapter 2, this account of who we grieve for and what grief is explains both the variety of persons we grieve for and the variety of emotions that grief elicits in us.

What good might come of grief understood in this light?

Let us return to the thought that grieving is an activity. I do not have any technical notion in mind by use of the term "activity." Earlier I offered the example of paying one's bills. Typical examples of activities are no less prosaic: organizing a meeting, playing a game, preparing a meal, drafting an e-mail. Grief, I have proposed, is an emotionally driven activity as opposed to an emotional *state* such as fear, anger, etc. We have already cataloged two ways in which activities differ from states. They tend to have longer duration and they are active in that they require, and are moved forward at least partially by, our agency—by our judgments, choices, and actions. The bill payer responds to the facts before her (facts about amounts due, due dates, etc.), makes judgments about how best to proceed, and then acts on those judgments (submitting online payments, for instance). This example illustrates two further features of activities. Activities have parts or stages. An activity can be broken down into additional tasks or actions that constitute the activity. Last, activities are purpose-driven. They have a purpose or a good at which they aim. Paying bills, organizing a meeting, and grieving have a point.

It is this last feature of grief—that it has a purpose or point—that holds the key to identifying the distinctive good of grief and thereby beginning to resolve the paradox of grief. For the good of an activity is a reflection of its purpose: An activity is success-ful, and thereby good for those who engage in it, when it realizes its purpose. The bill payer has succeeded in her activity just in case she has addressed the bills needing payment; the meeting organizer has succeeded in his activity just in case the invitees arrive and conduct their shared business effectively; etc. Like-wise, in the case of grief, whatever counts as successfully grieving will indicate the whereabouts of the distinctive good of grief. Our question now becomes: Given all the evidence we have about grief's nature, object, and so on, what purpose can plausi-bly be attributed to the activity of grieving?

Grief's purpose begins to emerge when we contrast grief with other emotional states. Compare (again) grief to fear. In typical cases, whatever fact prompts fear in us, fear discloses that fact's importance to us forthwith: This fact is a threat to ourselves or what we care about. The feeling of fear reveals the significance of its object more or less immediately and all at once. Fear thus fits a picture of the emotions wherein they are "on the spot" per-ceptions or judgments of what matters to us. Note that this need not mean that we immediately understand the object or what is fearful about it. We can after all interrogate our fears. (Why are we afraid of darkness anyway?) But fear rarely presents us with any deep challenge or puzzle about its objects.

On the other hand, grief is an activity that unfolds over time largely because it does not reveal the significance of its formal object in an immediate or direct way. Grief's material object, the death of someone who matters to our practical identity, is obvious to grieving persons. We quickly grasp what prompts our grief: because someone who matters to us has died. But fully coming to terms with grief's formal object, the relationship with the deceased that their death has transformed, is often trickier. For one, the amount of emotional "data" we have to wrestle with can be extensive. As I once put it, grief is our "psyche's way of instigating an emotional data dump."[12] As we observed in chapter 2, grief episodes involve many affective states—sadness or pain, of course, but also anger, guilt, anxiety, joy, etc. This emotional panoply makes what is happening to us while grieving harder to pin down. How, after all, can one and the same event result in a person sometimes feeling sadness, other times anger, other times anxiety, and so on? I proposed in chapter 2 that the various emotions we feel throughout a grief episode are our way of attending to the various elements of our relationship with the deceased. That we feel anxiety in the course of grieving informs us of something about our relationship to them (in all likelihood, that we felt a strong sense of attachment to them). That we feel anger in the course of grief informs us of something else about that relationship. So too for guilt, joy, or whatever other emotions occur within a grief episode. Each of these draws our attention to specific features of our relationships with deceased. Nevertheless, the plurality of emotions we feel in grief makes its object—exactly what we are grieving *about*—harder to pin down.

That grief is often unruly and unpredictable further adds to this challenge. As Lewis's grief for Joy attests, grief can be a roller coaster, a tumultuous, nonlinear, and intermittent process that ebbs and flows. Just when we may believe we have a handle on our loss, grief can offer us new, and even contradictory, evidence. As Didion describes in *The Year of Magical Thinking*, grief "comes in waves, paroxysms, sudden apprehensions that weaken the knees and blind the eyes and obliterate the dailiness of life."[13]

Earlier I suggested that grieving requires an agent to improvise in the manner of a musical performer. But arguably, the bereaved have a harder task than the musical improvisor. At least the improvisor can read ahead in the score and anticipate the forthcoming notes. A grieving person often cannot do much more than react to the unfolding of emotions as they come, improvising moment to moment.

The idea that grief thus generates bewilderment or perplexity not often found in other emotional states should not be surprising. For not only does grieving disclose a large quantity of emotional data, it discloses it haphazardly. Again, we do not struggle to understand the cause(s) of our grief. But we often struggle to understand what matters to us about those causes. As a result, our grasp of what matters to us about our relationship to the deceased is often tentative, a work in progress that can seem to have resolved itself only to resurface unexpectedly. Grief, Lewis observes, is "like a long valley, a winding valley where any bend may reveal a totally new landscape."[14] One of the most active areas of current grief research is how to categorize grief episodes that are ostensibly unhealthy for the individual, i.e., that are "pathological." Researchers disagree about both the nature and prevalence of pathological grieving (how often grief is "delayed," occurring significantly after the death that ultimately triggers grief, or "complicated," prolonged, or unusually arduous).[15] Nevertheless, all acknowledge that the grief process does not have the relatively simple dynamics of emotional states such as fear, wherein a person encounters some state of affairs, readily grasps the relevance of that state of affairs, and experiences the diminution of the relevant feelings as she becomes more distant from that state of affairs in time or space. As Jack Lewis's grief attests, grief can often throw us for a loop in ways that other emotional reactions do not. Getting a handle on the totality of a grief experience thus presents a challenge that other emotional states rarely do.

2. The Backward-Looking Dimension of Grief

I call this dimension of the activity of grieving its *backward-looking* dimension. In grieving, we look to the past relationship in order to make sense of the relationship we have lost. With the deaths of intimates in particular, we often lose a relationship with a multiplicity of different facets. Recall Lewis's grief for Joy, whom he described as his lover, confidant, critic, etc. Part of what puzzles and pains us in grief is how to describe, catalog, and synthesize the various ways in which a person's existence was central to our practical identities. The absence of those who matter enough to us to elicit grief is different from the absence of those who do not. Their absence is not a merely metaphysical fact. It is instead a fact of deep ethical (indeed, axiological) importance to our histories as individuals. We suffer in grief partly because another's death disrupts our practical identities.[16]

But the precise nature of this disruption is not necessarily transparent to us. Questions of love are particularly acute in this regard. Martha Nussbaum has emphasized our proclivity to deceive ourselves about love. We often have conflicted feelings "about who; and how; and when; and whether" we love. Our difficulty then becomes

> how in the midst of this confusion (and delight and pain) do we know what view of ourselves, what parts of ourselves, to trust? Which stories about the condition of the heart are the reliable ones and which the self-deceiving fictions? We find ourselves asking where, in this plurality of discordant voices with which we address ourselves on this topic of perennial self-interest, is the criterion of truth?[17]

Because grief's object is the relationship transformed by another's death, it can bring such questions of love to the forefront of our consciousness in a striking, even painful, way. Nussbaum draws upon Marcel Proust's *Remembrance of Things Past* to illustrate how grief can both raise and resolve questions of love. Proust's unnamed narrator is convinced that his love for Albertine is gone, until he receives word of her death. He then undergoes a painful surge of memories prompted by everyday events, at the conclusion of which his love for her strikes him like a nearly religious revelation. Proust's narrator is shocked by his suffering, but only because he had previously managed to obscure his love for Albertine from his own awareness. As Proust understood it, he "had been mistaken in thinking that I could see clearly into my own heart. But this knowledge, which the shrewdest perceptions of the mind would not have given me, had now been brought to me, hard, glittering, strange, like a crystallised salt, by the abrupt reaction of pain." Nussbaum traces such emotional dynamics to our tendency to develop habits that conceal the true nature of our relationships and why they matter to us. We become accustomed to our relationships, uncritically relying on them to ground our practical lives but also losing sight of our dependence on them. Nussbaum thus concludes that Proust's narrator had "been able to conclude that he is not in love with Albertine, in part because he is *used to her*."[18] Didion likewise wonders how her husband John's death could have happened "when everything was normal?"[19]

Grief shakes us in part because we tend to build our practical identities around the existence of other people, those whose existences are contingent, but then forget that fact. Grief thus brings the vulnerability, and ultimate contingency, of our practical identities into stark relief.[20] In the early stages of grief, disbelief is common: "I can't believe he/she/they are gone." Such statements are hard to parse. It may seem as if these statements express what Kübler-Ross believed to be the first stage of grief, namely, denial. But that does not seem accurate to these statements. The bereaved person is not asserting that she does *not* believe the deceased is dead.[21] Rather, such statements express a sense that their death is unfathomable. This disbelief marks a gap between the sheer recognition of the person's death and a full emotional engagement with their death. The death has not yet "sunk in." Rick Anthony Furtak offers a careful reconstruction of this moment between knowledge of the other's death and grief proper:

> Our opinion that this person has died, without the deeply upsetting feeling of grief, is akin to a tentative hypothesis that we have scarcely begun to acknowledge—it does not carry the force of a profound conviction, or of a vivid perceptual impression. If I have heard just now that someone I care about has passed away, I may be intellectually accepting the truth of this report without being fully aware of what it means. It is reasonable to conclude that I don't fully *know* about this person's death, because the thought of her death minus the feeling of passionate upheaval is not the same thought.[22]

In the backward-looking dimension of grief, we attempt to bridge this gap, from the fact *that* the person is dead to an appreciation of *who* is dead and *why* their deaths matter to us, a gap that opens up largely owing to the all-too-human tendency to ignore our reliance on others in our practical identities.[23] Because death transforms our relationship with the deceased, grief makes it no longer possible to take those relationships for granted, as death-averse beings like ourselves are prone to do. Grief is thus a form of emotional upheaval, upending those habits that, according to Proust and Nussbaum, can obscure the roles that others play in our practical identities.[24]

Not all the relationships for which we grieve are love relationships. But the fact that grief can lead to the interrogation of love
is a very stark example of the broader way in which grief involves
interrogation of the relationships in question. Grief affords us
evidence regarding the significance of those relationships[25]—in
the form of the sadness, anxiety, anger, etc., that we find ourselves undergoing in grief episodes—while also stoking puzzlement about that significance. Grief thus becomes an occasion
for asking "who were they to me?" Grief is therefore a privileged
epistemic route to our pasts. In grief's absence, we risk being
irreversibly alienated from our personal histories.[26]

3. The Forward-Looking Dimension of Grief

Yet grief is not focused solely on the past. In the "Dual Process"
model of grief elaborated by Margaret Stroebe and Henk Schut,
grieving individuals oscillate between the backward-looking
dimension of grief I have described, focused primarily on the
sense of loss, and a more prospective frame of mind they call
the "restoration orientation," in which individuals attempt to
reorient themselves in a world changed by the death of another.
In their view, negative emotions tend to dominate the backward-
looking dimension, whereas the restoration orientation generally involves more optimistic feelings. Crucially, Stroebe and
Schut deny that grief involves coming to terms with a past relationship only so that we can "move on." Rather, "rethinking and
replanning one's life in the face of bereavement" should also be
regarded as "an essential component of grieving."[27] This dimension of grieving is *forward-looking*, concerned primarily with
how a person's life will continue in the absence of the deceased.
As I proposed in chapter 2, the death of someone in whom we
have invested our practical identities instigates a relationship

crisis with the deceased. Their death alters the patterns of, and possibilities for, our relating to them. We are thus compelled to alter our relationships with them.[28]

We therefore face not only the *retrospective* challenge of grasping the significance of that relationship as it was when the person was still alive. We simultaneously face the *prospective* challenge of determining how that relationship will fit into our future life. We may continue to have our practical identities invested in the deceased. But there may be some concerns, projects, and commitments we will need to jettison because the deceased can no longer play the special role they played in those concerns, projects, and commitments. (It may no longer make sense to maintain a large house for only one.) Others can perhaps continue but may need to be revamped or reconceptualized to account for their absence. (The annual New Year's Eve party may need to be catered instead of home cooked.) Perhaps some concerns, projects, and commitments become more available or attractive in light of their death. (She always got seasick on boat trips anyway.) But unless the bereaved is delusional or in extreme denial, some choices will have to be made regarding what life looks like in the world without the deceased. Prior to the deceased's death, such choices were largely irrelevant. But with their death they become unavoidable, even urgent. And many grieving persons report simply not knowing "how to go on." Ami Harbin aptly treats grief as a paradigm example of a moral "disorientation," a "temporally extended" major life experience that makes it "difficult for individuals to know how to go on," often involving "feeling deeply out of place, unfamiliar, or not at home."[29] The disorientation associated with grief can feel like a "loss of coordinates,"[30] as a person whose existence helped establish our practical bearings can no longer provide that same guidance. Colin Parkes observes that "when someone dies, a whole set of assumptions about the world that relied upon the other person for their validity are suddenly invalidated."[31] The forward-looking dimension of grief is our effort to identify how, if at all, our relationship with the deceased will continue as a result of the change in background realities that their death has wrought. This change is the focus of much of the emotional attention that is central to grief. Our emotional attention is drawn to the deceased individual because we are, however inchoately, attempting to ascertain how we can and will relate to her now and in the future.

Stroebe and Schut call their view a dual process theory, apparently seeing what I have called the forward- and backward-looking dimensions of grief activity as largely separate. However, I believe it is more fruitful to view these as two elements of a single activity.[32] First, we can acquire evidence or insight relevant to one of these while engaging in the other. In considering how one wishes to live in light of another's death, we may reflect on what our lives are missing since that person's death. And in reflecting on the significance of our relationship with the deceased, we may draw upon our efforts to live without them to understand what they were to us. More deeply, grief can be seen as corresponding to a *narrative disruption* in our lives. I am skeptical that grief must take the form of a narrative. However, grief clearly can serve as a pivotal juncture in our life narratives, the stories we use to account for our choices and actions. The death of a person central to our practical identity will mean, in various ways and in varying degrees, that our narratives will have to adapt. We will have to choose and act differently than we might have had their death not occurred when and as it did. But narrative building involves looking both backward and forward at once: In fashioning a coherent story, a narrator must see it in its totality, and any given point within the story acquires its coherence from its relation to other points within it. To the extent then that grieving has both backward- and forward-looking dimensions, it can be seen as an activity of revising one's existing life narrative in light of the death of one of that narrative's principal characters. The questions "who were they to me?" and "how can I go on?" are thus pursued in the service of a larger question: "who shall I be in light of who I have been?"

4. Self-Knowledge and the Resolution of Practical Identity Crises

I have described grief as flowing from a relationship crisis with the deceased. In some grief episodes, this crisis will be, well, a *crisis*, a serious, long-term effort to grapple with the significance, both retrospective and prospective, the deceased person has for our practical identities. In other cases, such as the death of a celebrity whom one admired, the "crisis" may be minor, resolving itself in an afternoon. But no matter the magnitude of the relationship crisis, this is simultaneously an *identity* crisis. For in interrogating our relationship with the deceased, both in terms of what it meant to us and what role it will play in our futures, we are also figuring out who we are. Their deaths have made it such that our prior practical identi- ties, in which the deceased played a pivotal role, cannot be intelligibly endorsed or pursued. They must therefore be amended or updated. Our "realistic expectations regarding interaction with another person are irreparably altered by that person's death," as Kathleen Higgins observes, "but one's sense of identity continues to be constructed in part on the basis of one's relationship to that person."[33]

Who are we to become, now that a central facet of who we were is no longer so? Grief involves losses *to* ourselves, yes. But many grieving persons also report a loss *of* self, an alienation from their familiar patterns of feeling, choosing, and acting.[34] "I feel like I've lost a part of myself," they commonly say. Some even describe this loss of self in physical terms, as a kind of disability. Lewis analogized his new condition to an amputation.

> To say the patient is getting over it after an operation for appendicitis is one thing; after he's had his leg off it is quite another. After that operation either the wounded stump heals or the man dies. If it heals, the fierce, continuous pain will stop. Presently he'll get back his strength and be able to stump about on his wooden leg. He has "got over it." But he will probably have recurrent pains in the stump all his life, and perhaps pretty bad ones; and he will always be a one-legged man.[35]

This sense of no longer fully knowing who one is, of having lost one's way in a previously familiar emotional environment, hints at where the purpose, and the good, of grief reside: If grief represents a kind of ignorance of self—a condition of no longer recognizing oneself *as* oneself—then we can expect that grief's successful resolution will involve a *reconstruction* of one's knowledge of self. The good in grief, I propose, is *self-knowledge*.

Let us imagine how this might have played out in Jack Lewis's case. Lewis was saddened and distressed partially by the loss of the various goods that Joy provided him (companionship, etc.). He found himself unprepared for many of the emotions his grief episode prompted, especially the fear, embarrassment, and laziness. Joy's absence permeated nearly all of his day-do-day experience, "like the sky, spread over everything."[36] Yet when not distracted by work or other preoccupations, Lewis has intrusive thoughts, a "a vague sense of wrongness, of something amiss," a world "flat, shabby, worn-out looking."[37]

And as we have seen, Lewis's emotional condition was also bewildered and disoriented, a kind of estrangement from the world he had shared with Joy. He feels himself somehow transformed. But Lewis's estrangement was also an estrangement from himself and his previous practical identity. Old habits, places, and activities did not resonate as they did before. Even his own body seemed alien to him.

> Bathing, dressing, sitting down and getting up again, even lying in bed, will all be different. His whole way of life will be changed. All sorts of pleasures and activities that he once took for granted will have to be simply written off. At present I am learning to get about on crutches. Perhaps I shall presently be given a wooden leg. But I shall never be a biped again.[38]

Lewis's grief involved both of its dimensions: He reflected back on his history with Joy, but also attempted to ascertain how his life might look without his irreplaceable wife. He struggles to fully articulate Joy's place in his previous practical identity and where, if at all, she fits into the new practical identity he must now craft for himself. Indeed, for Lewis, grieving brought almost every element of his practical identity into question: the importance of his own scholarly work, his public image, even his Christian faith.

The self-knowledge we may achieve through grief is not pedestrian, the sort of self-knowledge wherein we know that we are wearing a hat, that our left ring finger hurts, that we are thirsty, etc. Rather, grief catalyzes what Quassim Cassam has called "substantial self-knowledge," knowledge of our "values, emotions, abilities, and of what makes one happy."[39] As animals that live in community with other humans, our self-understandings and practical identities depend in large measure on the social world we share with others. Grief reflects just how deeply embedded our practical identities are within that shared social world. Those identities assume the existence of others to play various roles in our projects, commitments, and concerns, and when those others die, they cannot play precisely those same roles. Their deaths jar us out of the emotional complacency that, as Nussbaum and Proust emphasized, we all too readily fall into. As Solomon observes, others' deaths remind us of our vulnerability and dependence upon others,[40] facts we are rather prone to forget in the hustle and bustle of everyday life. Yet when we manage to emerge from grief with a rejuvenated practical identity and a more stable sense of self, this is because grief afforded us a richer knowledge of who we have been and who we seek to be. Self-knowledge is therefore the purpose, and the good, of grief. Grief is thus a surprisingly philosophical enterprise. For it demands that we wrestle with the question at the core of philosophy inquiry: How shall I live?

Of course, grief is not the only opportunity in life for substantial self-knowledge. Yet it is an especially crucial source of self-knowledge. Especially in instances where grief is strong or prolonged, we encounter a wide range of emotions, and accordingly, a wide range of facts about our relationship with the deceased and about our practical identities. Few other life experiences reveal a similarly wide vista on who we are. Furthermore, the fact that grief is emotionally intense makes it a powerful motivator for self-knowledge. Emotions motivate reflection, deliberation, and action, and in grief, it is difficult to avoid its component emotions. For grief, as we established in chapter 2, is a species of sustained emotional *attention* to one's relationship with the deceased, a relationship that cannot continue in the same guise as before. This emotional attention galvanizes our efforts to make sense of that relationship retrospectively and prospectively. Lastly, grief provides us with an opportunity for self-knowledge at pivotal moments in life. We seem to need the self-knowledge that grief fosters in order to proceed forward, and in its absence, there is the danger that we become mired in the past, lingering over a relationship with the deceased that we can no longer sustain in its previous form, or that we simply "move on" without incorporating this relationship into our prospective practical identity. Hence, the self-knowledge grief enables is likely to be especially valuable to us given where it occurs within our biographies. Grief's role as both a powerful source and motivator of substantial self-knowledge, as well as where it occurs within our life experience, indicates that grief is distinctive among possible avenues to self-knowledge. At the very least, I cannot imagine another life experience that could provide the same potential for self-knowledge as grief does.

Let us now address three objections to my claim that self-knowledge is the distinctive good of grief.

5. Objection 1: The Self Is Not Static

Some may blanch at calling the purpose or good of grief "self-knowledge." That term may imply that the self is a static entity, an unchanging set of facts that can be mastered once and for all. Yet in calling self-knowledge the good of grief, I do not imply that the self is a stable object. As an emotionally driven activity, grief involves several emotional states, each of which motivates us to seek both corroboration for the concerns those emotions represent and reasons to care about those concerns.[41] A person who experiences anger in the course of grieving may find this anger puzzling or unexpected. In trying to process her anger, she will undertake a descriptive task, trying to identify what about her relationship with the deceased causes such anger, and an evaluative task, trying to assess whether that anger is warranted. In making sense of our emotions, particularly when they are unexpected or anomalous, we operate from the presumption that those emotions will turn out to be justified—that we not only do feel as we do but that we *should* feel as we do. That presumption may end up being overturned—the grieving person's anger, she may conclude, is unjustified. But even that conclusion represents a parcel of practical self-knowledge (that, say, she should attempt to incorporate the deceased into her future life and to the extent possible, free herself from this anger). As a "questioning" emotion, grief invites just that kind of dual inquiry. And what we come to know when we grieve successfully is what elements our practical identity will contain now that we must live without the deceased other for whom we grieve—what projects, concerns, and commitments will orient us into the future. Identifying those elements can involve both inventorying our past projects, concerns, and commitments, as well as considering new ones. Our search for a new practical identity, one adapted to the new circumstances established by another's death, is a fundamentally practical enterprise. For in the course of grief, we are seeking a practical identity that we can *endorse*. To echo Korsgaard, practical identities are not just statements of fact about ourselves. They are descriptions under which we value ourselves that provide us reasons for action and guide choice. Many elements of the practical identities we have prior to the deaths of those for whom we grieve will survive the reconfiguration of our practical identity that we undertake while grieving. Other elements will be more novel. Jack Lewis, for instance, continued to teach at

Cambridge, but took on the new role of "single parent" to the two sons Joy had from a previous marriage. But the self that we may better come to know through grief is not static.

Admittedly, the term "self-knowledge" may only awkwardly capture the good in question. Perhaps "self-understanding" or "self-insight" ring truer. All the same, that self-knowledge is the purpose and the distinctive good of grief fully accords with the experience of grief.

6. Objection 2: Over-Intellectualization

Grief is among the emotions that aim at "disclosing something true."[42] To evade grief, or to grieve halfheartedly or in bad faith, is therefore bad for us because it deprives us of one of our greatest opportunities for self-knowledge. Only in rare cases, I suggest, would it be sensible to forego this opportunity in order to avoid the emotional tumult of grief.

Yet some may sense that calling the good of grief self-knowledge is to *intellectualize* grief. On my view, successful grieving culminates in a desirable epistemic condition, self-knowledge. It might appear that this turns a fundamentally emotional process into a fundamentally cerebral one. Few grieving individuals are likely to view their grieving in the terms I have described, and it seems especially unlikely that the "naïve" bereaved are pursuing self-knowledge through grief. Is it really credible that a child grieving the death of a pet is in pursuit of self-knowledge, for instance?

Several points suffice to answer this objection. First, the objection may reflect too easy an acceptance of a dichotomy between emotion and reason. Emotions are not simply "dumb" states, disconnected from larger facts outside our minds. They have a central role in generating and refining our rational judgments. We have emphasized that grief is a form of emotionally laden attention that generally involves multiple different forms of affect (sadness, anger, guilt, etc.) directed at the relationship one had with the deceased individual for whom one grieves. Grief thus informs us about what matters to us, both shaping and being shaped by our beliefs. The objection thus overlooks how emotion and rational judgment interact. Furthermore, despite the purpose of grief being a state of knowledge rather than some emotional condition, the emotions remain indispensable to our ability to gain such knowledge. That self-knowledge is grief's purpose or good does not drain grief of its emotionality. Rather, self-knowledge explains how the emotions we undergo in grief cohere and contribute to successful grieving.

Second, imagination can play a part in grieving and contribute to self-knowledge. As we have seen, the other's death does not so much terminate our relationship to them but necessitate its reconfiguration. And the exploration of that relationship and how it might continue can sometimes take the form of artistic or creative expression (for instance, journaling, scrapbooking, and the like). Much of our engagement with the deceased will be "imaginal," i.e., interactions in which we envision and engage with the deceased dialogically or conversationally.[43] These interactions are not veridical; unless we accept the existence of the afterlife, we are not *literally* in conversation with the deceased. But neither are they imaginary in the sense of being fictitious. Imaginal engagement involves drawing upon one's actual, lived experience with the deceased to hypothesize communion with them. Such imaginal engagement can sustain what Matthew Ratcliffe has usefully called "second personal" relationships with the deceased.[44] Suppose that a bereaved person sees a film and is prompted to wonder what the person she grieves for might have thought of it. From her internal perspective, this wondering could be third-personal: "what would he have thought?" But this wondering could be imaginally directed at the deceased in a second-personal way: "what would *you* have thought?" This imaginal engagement may be useful in both the backward- and forward-looking dimensions of grief, allowing us both to grasp our prior relationship with the deceased and to develop a new relationship with them.[45] Imaginal engagement with the deceased is to some extent intellectual, inasmuch as it relies upon existing beliefs about, and experiences with, them. But it is in another way imaginative, inasmuch as we are attempting to extend that knowledge to new phenomena, hypothesizing about what our interactions with the deceased would be like. Modern technologies make available novel forms of this imaginative engagement. Recently, chatbots have been developed using data from deceased persons' online interactions. Such chatbots use predictive analytics to mimic the responses the deceased person would have given to living interlocutors. It would be unfortunate if such chatbots supplanted other forms of grieving or if bereaved persons understood these interactions "supernaturally," taking the deceased person to actually be present behind the chatbot. Nevertheless, such technologies offer genuine opportunities to engage the deceased at an imaginal level and establish continuing bonds with them.[46]

Last, we must distinguish between grief having self-knowledge as its purpose and grieving having self-knowledge among its *aims*. Like any activity, grieving has parts, component experiences or states, through which we progress. And these parts are likely to have aims specific to them that need not coincide with self-knowledge as the purpose. The bill payer or the meeting organizer has a larger purpose, but they need not have that purpose in mind during the various component parts of these activities. They will instead have smaller, subsidiary aims in mind as the activity unfolds over time (organizing the bills by due date, keeping a running account balance, etc.). The purposes of an activity are often realized not by our aiming at them, but by aiming at the various parts of the activity. So too, I suggest, for grief: Few are likely to grieve consciously pursuing self-knowledge. They instead have aims associated with parts of the grieving process, such as addressing sadness or longing, dealing with legal matters arising from the other's death, establishing new patterns of domestic life, for example. The bereaved person's engagement with each of these parts can contribute to the ultimate purpose of grief—self-knowledge. But if so, this will not likely be because the bereaved person sought self-knowledge in any of the stages of grief or even through grieving as a whole. Self-knowledge is instead a *by-product* of successful grieving rather than its express aim. The purpose of grief may therefore be "intellectual" without its aims being intellectual. In this respect, successful or healthy grieving may be better pursued indirectly. To commit oneself to grieve in order to attain self-knowledge may prove counterproductive, in the way that committing to living a more spontaneous life is counterproductive.

7. Objection 3: Grief Is Not Self-Focused

Other critics may worry that I have represented grief as overly *self-focused*. Many of the thoughts we have while grieving are not about ourselves and our own states. They are instead directed primarily at the deceased person. We are, after all, grieving *for* them. "From the vantage point of a grieving . . . person, one's affective state is outwardly oriented: it is *about* some aspect of the world."[47] Critics may allege that to assert that grief has a state of oneself (self-knowledge) as its purpose distorts grief, making it out to be an egoistic, even narcissistic, condition.

The objection is not off base in observing that much of our mental focus in grieving is not on ourselves but on others. But here I suggest that appearances are deceiving.

Many of our emotions concern facts outside of ourselves. Fear and anger are directed at facts out in the world; late to catch a bus, we fear that we will miss it, but once we see it pull away, we are angry that we have missed it. But other emotions can be directed *at* ourselves. For instance, we can feel shame at who we are or what we have done. In that case, shame is something we feel concerning ourselves. So too for shame's opposite, pride. We feel pride at who we are or what we have done. Such emotions are possible because human consciousness includes self-consciousness. We can perceive the world around us, and so can feel emotions such as fear and anger at events in the world we perceive around us. But we also have a sense of self, and so can have emotions about the self. When experienced in these ways, such emotions are *reflexive*.[48]

The objection at hand can be restated in these terms: I have depicted grief as concerned with ourselves, and in particular with our practical identities and the ways in which another's death exerts pressure on those identities. But grief and the various emotional states that comprise it are not reflexive. We do not grieve about ourselves. Rather, grief draws our attention to the deceased.

To some extent, my response to this objection has been anticipated earlier, in chapter 1. We noted there that we do not grieve all deaths. Rather, grief is selective, prompted only by those whose deaths matter to us in a specific way. I have argued that the way they matter is by their having been incorporated into our practical identities. But unless we stood in some sort of important relation to the deceased, it would be difficult to explain the selectivity. Grief must be egocentric, concerned with how others' deaths affect us, lest we have no way of accounting for why we typically grieve our siblings and spouses but not our postal carriers or periodontists. And an egocentric response is, unsurprisingly, a self-focused one, oriented at what we the bereaved have lost.

Still, my opponents may wonder how to square this argument with the fact that so many of our thoughts, in the midst of grief, are about the person we grieve and not (apparently) about ourselves.

Recall my suggestion that grief represents a kind of emotional attention. Like grief itself, attention is selective, that is, attention is our capacity to devote our mental resources to some facts *rather than* others. In grieving, our attention (I have argued) is guided by our relationship with the deceased and how they played an essential role in our practical identity. And not every fact about the deceased matters to our practical identity and our relationship to the deceased. Take memories, for example. Memory is itself a way of paying attention to the past and is notoriously selective. Rarely is our memory "photographic," able to re-represent every detail of some important event or experience. Our emotions themselves influence what and how we remember, so that we tend primarily to remember emotionally salient facts.[49] A grieving person may have many vivid memories of the deceased, but what she can remember is limited by what she was present for, and what she is likely to remember is what is emotionally salient to her—in my terms, those events that provide her the picture of the deceased that she has incorporated into her practical identity.

But note that a person's memories are memories of her own experiences even though she does not appear within those experiences. We largely "drop out" out of view in our own memories. Except: Our memories are emotionally valenced. We often remember the emotions we experienced during past events. In fact, these emotions are why we remember much of what we do. Memory is thus often a mirror in which we are invisible except for our emotions.

What is true of memory is true of grief more generally: What appear to be thoughts concerned with the deceased are, at root, concerned with ourselves. We engage with facts in which the deceased are implicated but only because our practical identities make those facts relevant to our relationship with the deceased. And we only think we are not present in our thoughts about the deceased because we are not present as the objects of those thoughts. But we are very much present as the emotional subjects of those thoughts. The idea that grief is not self-focused or reflexive is therefore an illusion due to our not appreciating our emotional presence in the thoughts we have about the deceased persons we grieve.

8. Healthy Grief: Neither Moving On Nor Letting Go

This book does not aim to be therapeutic in any direct sense. Yet simply understanding better our own situation as we grieve can be a source of solace or reassurance. And the account of grief's goodness provided here offers an attractive picture of what healthy grieving might look like. Healthy grieving does not aim, as Freud believed, at severing our ties with the deceased.[50] For successful grief does not entail the cessation of the bereaved's relationship with the deceased. Our relationships to the dead often can and should continue, emotionally and practically. Grief's culmination is thus more than "moving on" or "letting go." But neither does my account imply the popular view that we are best served "holding onto" or tending to our grief indefinitely, as if it were an indelible wound.[51] My account allows that grief's conclusion is sometimes provisional—that memories of the deceased can return well after the event of their death, sometimes prompted by unexpected and highly specific stimuli such as voices or colors. But this does not imply that we should hope that grief never abates. Grieving well, as Tony Walter has put it, enables us to fashion a "durable biography" that integrates the memory of the deceased individual into our practical identities.[52] Good grief—grief that achieves what is distinctly good in grief—is not a matter of letting go or holding on, but of *building from* one's past relationship with the deceased. My account acknowledges that grief generally comes to at least a tentative conclusion, and when that conclusion coincides with self-knowledge, grief has contributed to a well-lived life. Grief often ends, with no warning or notification from our psyches. But nothing in my account suggests that bringing grief to an end is up to us. The conclusion of grief need not temporally coincide with the achievement of self-knowledge, nor will we always recognize that this good has been attained. And achieving this good may demand fortitude and occasional effort. But we will have less reason to regret grieving if self-knowledge is in the offing, and the grounds for recommending grief to others as a central part of the human condition become less obscure.

9. Resilience, Recovery, and Regret

Recently, several philosophers have concluded that we may have reason to regret how grief typically unfolds. A number of studies have shown that we "recover" from grief more rapidly than we expect. Most people return to their previous baseline of subjective well-being about six months after the deaths of their spouses, for example.[53] Several philosophers have found our apparent "resilience" in the face of grief a troubling commentary on our relationships with those who matter to us. They differ regarding exactly what the trouble is: Dan Moller considers whether this resilience might show that those individuals never mattered to us in the first place, or that without the feelings of sadness associated with grief, we are cut off from the primary way of relating to the deceased and understanding how they mattered to us.[54] Erica and Ryan Preston-Roedder worry that it represents a kind of desertion of the deceased.[55] Aaron Smuts concludes that, absent this sadness, we will come to no longer care about the deceased and thus suffer a "death of self."[56]

I think that these worries about resilience and regret are largely misplaced. This is not because grief can never be regrettable. I worry, for example, that Jack Lewis's grief was mostly for nought. His memoir contained little indication that he achieved the self-knowledge I have argued is the good in grief. As *A Grief Observed* proceeds, Joy progressively recedes from view. Lewis finds solace by taking a more impartial view of his situation. He asks, "From the rational point of view, what new factor has H.'s death introduced into the problem of the universe? What grounds has it given me for doubting all that I believe?"[57] His answer to these questions is, essentially, no grounds at all. Jack concludes that he ought to be grateful to God for having made it possible for him to have the gift of true love for Joy, a love that mirrors his love for God. His focus thus shifts from his relationship with Joy to his relationship with God. This shift is perhaps predictable given Lewis's Christian convictions and interest in theological matters. But he never confronts the shame and despair that Joy's death prompts or engages with his shock and surprise at the emotions he felt in grief. Nor does he interrogate "the bath of self-pity, the wallow, the loathsome sticky-sweet pleasure of indulging" in his grief, an indulgence that disgusted and appalled him.[58] To my mind, Jack Lewis retreated from his grief for Joy to a more psychologically comfortable but emotionally sterile landscape, and in so doing, probably deprived himself of valuable self-knowledge.

So grief *can* be regrettable. But I doubt that the resilience these philosophers are anxious about is a particular cause for regret. For one, some of their anxieties rest on a mistaken picture of how death affects the relationship between the bereaved and the deceased. As we have seen, in most cases, the bereaved continue their relationships with the deceased. Indeed, grief seems healthiest when the bereaved are able to continue their relationship to the deceased under the new terms necessitated by the latter's death.[59] Thus, the Preston-Roedders' concern that unexpectedly rapid reductions in sadness, our "recovery from" or resilience in the face of grief, amount to a desertion of the deceased is not plausible. For we generally do not desert the deceased. So too for Smuts's concern that this resilience entails that we no longer care for the beloved and therefore suffer a "death of" the self defined by such care. I have argued that their death requires a transformation of the self (i.e., a revision or updating of one's practical identity) in response to the transformation of our relationship with the deceased necessitated by their deaths. But this transformation need not involve the deceased no longer mattering to us. They simply cannot matter precisely as they did before their deaths.

Moller believes that this resilience dissolves our primary epistemic link with the deceased. Our "affective immune system" enables us to recover from intense emotional loss too quickly. The upshot of this "recovery," according to Moller, is that our reactions no longer track the significance of the person we have lost. "What we have lost remains the same," he claims, "even as the intensity of our response begins its meteoric dive toward the baseline where it no longer seems to reflect the horror of what has happened."[60] The result is that we lose sight of how the deceased matter to us, and all the more, we are deprived of "insight into our own condition,"[61] that is, we suffer a kind of emotional detachment from what mattered to us about the deceased.

Moller reaches a conclusion about grief's value strikingly similar to my own—that it consists in grief's capacity to provide us insight into our own condition, i.e., self-knowledge. And we shall explore further (in chapter 5) how grief that ends too soon could be regrettable in much the way that Moller proposes. But Moller's own argument for why we should regret our resilience rests on too narrow a conception of the experience of grief.

If the sadness we feel in the course of grief were the *entirety* of grief, it might be regrettable that this sadness diminishes so as to sever us from what matters to us about those we grieve for. But as we have seen, sadness is not all there is to the activity of grieving. Grief also involves other emotional states, such as anxiety, guilt, joy, anger, and the like. And these states, no less than sadness, keep us "in touch" with the object of our grief. Very often, these other emotions will endure longer than the sadness will, in which case we have "recovered" from the other's death insofar as our lives are no longer weighed down by sadness. Nevertheless, the emotions other than sadness that are associated with grief provide us ample opportunity to continue to gain insight into our own condition through grieving. And if I am correct, this continued engagement is precisely what we should hope will occur, and when it occurs so as yield substantial self-knowledge, it ought not be a cause for regret. Whether we ought to regret the resilience or recovery to which Moller refers becomes a complex and contingent matter, based on whether the grief experience as a whole generates self-knowledge.[62]

10. What Good Is Self-Knowledge?

Note that, on my view, the good in grief is not rooted in its *feeling* good. In fact, grief may *have* to feel bad in order to generate the self-knowledge that can make it good. Of course, some may shrug at my conclusion that grief's distinctive good resides in how it fosters substantial self-knowledge. What, they may ask, is good about such self-knowledge?

I cannot exhaustively examine what makes self-knowledge good for us here. But to begin, notice that self-knowledge clearly has *instrumental* value to us. We need to know ourselves—our beliefs, desires, aspirations—in order to achieve much of what we want. We also need self-knowledge to rationally seek self-improvement. If we wish to make ourselves better morally, or to improve our skills or habits, we benefit from knowing our current state of moral virtue, our current skills or habits, etc. After all, changing some state of affairs nearly always demands knowledge of that state of affairs and how it may be susceptible or resistant to change. Knowledge is power; self-knowledge is a species of power governing ourselves, and so serves our ends just as any other form of power does.

In the particular case of grief, I would also suggest that self-knowledge enables us to achieve a desirable psychological condition. When we attain the self-knowledge grief affords us, our lives have a greater level of autobiographical coherence or integrity. From our standpoint in the present, our lives as a whole make greater sense. The deaths of those in whom we had our practical identities invested have been incorporated into our current practical identities, and to the extent that our current practical identities survive into the future, they are invested in our future lives as well. Grief that culminates in self-knowledge thus enables us to avoid alienation or fragmentation of our sense of self.

Yet self-knowledge has value beyond empowering us to attain our ends and achieve a desirable condition of autobiographical coherence or integrity. Indeed, self-knowledge is intrinsically valuable, worthwhile for its own sake.[63] Here's why:

Except in rare instances, we love ourselves. We care for ourselves for own sake; from our points of view, our fates are not just the fate of *someone*. They are the fate of us, and because of this, we are deeply, and perhaps unavoidably, invested in them.[64]

We also love others, caring for them for their own sake. But it seems contrary to love for others to not seek out knowledge of who they are below the surface—knowledge of their desires, emotional makeup, commitments, projects, and the like. Suppose that Tom claims to love Ursula, but Tom has no curiosity at all about who Ursula is. We would have reason to doubt Tom's professed love for Ursula. In particular, we would worry that for Tom, his interest in knowledge of Ursula is circumscribed by what he needs to know in order to care *for himself*—that what he perceives himself as needing to know about Ursula is what he needs to know about her in order to effectively pursue his own ends. His indifference toward knowing Ursula may indicate that he has instrumentalized Ursula rather than caring for her for her own sake. If Tom knew Ursula well, he could of course be more effective in caring for her. He would be better able to support her in her endeavors, would be less likely to frustrate or annoy her, would buy her better birthday gifts, and so on. So Tom's disinterest in knowing Ursula is instrumentally *dis*valuable to Ursula.

That Tom's lack of curiosity about Ursula fails Ursula is not the sole basis for criticizing Tom, though. The yearning to be loved is, among other things, a yearning to be seen in our fullness, to be understood—in other words, to be *known*. And we wish to be known by others not only so that they can serve our ends better. Rather, others knowing us is the basis of our being *cherished* by those who ostensibly love us. In cherishing us, those who love us treat us as objects of contemplation, attention, and appreciation. This stance, in turn, makes our natures more evident to them and enables them, to the extent possible, to identify with our consciousness.[65] Knowing someone we love is therefore not valuable only insofar as it makes us better able to care for them. It is in fact an intrinsically valuable way of caring for them.

What then of self-love and self-knowledge? What Nussbaum said about love for another applies in a limited way to self-love. Exactly who we love when we love ourselves can be opaque to us. In achieving self-knowledge, we bring the focus of that love into sharper relief, allowing us to cherish a person who, despite living with us night and day, can sometimes seem like a stranger. Self-knowledge enriches self-love, and just as knowing another is an intrinsically valuable way of caring about them, so too is knowing oneself an intrinsically valuable way of caring about a self with whom we stand in a loving relationship.

Hence, if (as I have argued in this chapter) we have reasons to recommend grief to those we care about for their own sake because grief can foster self-knowledge, self-knowledge is both instrumentally and intrinsically valuable; and if we care about ourselves for our own sake, then we have reasons to recommend grief to ourselves and to be grateful for grief as an opportunity for self-knowledge.

11. A Partial Resolution of the Paradox

A resolution to the paradox of grief is at hand: Although grief is painful, there is a distinctive good to be had in grief—self-knowledge—that can justify our belief that we ourselves are better off being susceptible to grief, unlike Camus's protagonist Meursault, as well as explaining why we should recommend grief to others. As we shall see in the next chapter, a full resolution of the paradox requires further investigation of the pain associated with grief. All the same, that self-knowledge is the good of grief gives considerably more substance to the belief in its value than popular appeals to vague goods such as "closure" or "coming to terms" with another's death.

CHAPTER FOUR

Making Good
on the Pain

Recall the paradox of grief:

- Grief feels bad, and so should be avoided or lamented.
- Grief is valuable such that we (and others) ought not
  avoid it altogether and should be grateful that we grieve.

Astute readers will notice that chapter 3 focused entirely on justifying the second claim, that grief is valuable. We concluded that grief's value consists in its capacity to be a distinctive source of self-knowledge.

But my conclusion that grief can yield a distinctive good is compatible with grief's being sufficiently bad—and, in particular, sufficiently *painful*—that it turns out to be bad on the whole. Grief, we noted in the introduction, is among the most stressful of life events. That grief can generate the good of self-knowledge may therefore fall short of showing that grief's pains are worth the trouble of attaining self-knowledge. By way of comparison, there may be some goods that flow from imprisonment or unemployment. But these goods hardly seem weighty or important enough when compared to the "bads" of imprisonment or unemployment for us to recommend these experiences to those we care about or for us to conclude that we should be grateful for the "opportunity" to be imprisoned or unemployed. Why shouldn't the same pessimistic conclusions hold for grief?

A full resolution of the paradox of grief therefore requires examining grief's pains, and especially how those pains relate to grief and to self-knowledge that I have proposed grief is especially well-suited to provide. This chapter considers several ways we might understand this relation before arriving at what I take to be the most plausible account of it. According to that account, grieving can make the pains of grief *good pains*—while still being undeniably painful.

One initial caveat: A satisfactory resolution of the paradox of grief need not show that each and every episode of grief, taking into account their respective goods and bads, is good for the bereaved. The activity of grieving may not yield the good of self-knowledge, as we noted in the previous chapter. The resolution of the paradox of grief only necessitates showing that *many* grief episodes are beneficial to the bereaved.

1. Masochism

One way to resolve the paradox of grief would be to show that the apparent psychological pains of grief are not straightforward instances of pain. And one way pain may deviate from the standard picture is if the pain is masochistic.

It is tempting to think that pain and pleasure are opposed and exclusive states—that any pleasant state is not painful and vice versa. But that is not the case. Aristotle describes anger as a mixture of pleasure and pain: Anger feels bad but this anger coexists with the delight of imagining revenge on the individual who wronged us.[1] And as Hume pointed out, many of us actively seek out and take pleasure in genres such as horror movies, despite the fact that they cause anxiety or fear.[2] Colin Klein offers other examples where pleasure and pain coexist: getting a deep tissue massage, wiggling a loose tooth, or jumping into icy water as part of a "polar bear" swim.[3]

Masochistic pleasure is difficult to understand, but it seems to involve the amalgamation of pain and pleasure within a given experience. Crucially, masochism does not involve experiencing pain *in order to acquire* subsequent pleasure. Masochism is instead a state in which sensations of pleasure and pain coexist in relation to the same object or situation. Klein suggests that the pains in question themselves have a pleasant quality, rooted in the fact that the pain pushes individuals to the edge of what they can endure. This is why, Klein argues, the masochistic condition of experiencing pleasure and pain simultaneously does not arise in contexts where people are undergoing mild or easily tolerable pain (a dull ache in one's finger, say).

Could we view the pains of grief in masochistic terms? If so, then we might be able to dissolve the paradox of grief. If grief were a masochistic pain, then whether or not (as I argued in the previous chapter) grief is good because it is a distinctive source of self-knowledge, the psychological pains of grief are both bad for being painful but also good for the bereaved in the way that masochistic pleasure is good. But if this is so, there may be no paradox here: Masochistic pain is not wholly bad—indeed, it is pleasurable too—and so should not be avoided or lamented.

As we shall see in sections 4 and 5, I am sympathetic to the proposal that grief may have features that render its pains not straightforwardly bad. But I doubt that the pains of grief are instances of masochism.

One problem here is that grief varies in its intensity and duration. Extremely arduous grief episodes, typified by Jack Lewis's grieving in response to Joy Davidman's death, may push people to the emotional edge, portending mental breakdown and the like. If Klein is correct that masochistic pleasure is limited to pains that push us to the limits of our endurance, then those undergoing especially severe grief may be undergoing masochism. But as we observed in section 3.9, most episodes of grief are not this severe or arduous. The pains of grief abate more quickly and fully than we expect. Thus, if the psychological pains of grief are parts of masochistic experience, these pains will only be good for the bereaved in the minority of cases where grief is especially emotionally taxing or prolonged.

More fundamentally, I am not aware of any evidence that when individuals are psychologically anguished due to grief, they are simultaneously undergoing some form of pleasure. Of course, some of the affective states we undergo during grief are pleasant: joy, peace, love for the deceased individual for whom we grieve. But the pain of grief—the sadness, sorrow, and so forth—does not co-occur with some pleasant sensation. So we cannot make sense of how grief can be worthwhile despite being painful by claiming that the pain is masochistic in character, a pain in which we nevertheless take pleasure.

2. Pain versus Suffering

A second way to show that the pains of grief are not straightforward instances of pain is to propose that while they are genuinely painful, they fall short of outright *suffering*. Michael Brady, for example, argues that there is more to suffering than simply undergoing an unpleasant sensation. To suffer, a person must also desire that the unpleasant sensation cease. And, according to Brady, not every unpleasant sensation is one that we are especially concerned that it cease. A person engaged in a long, lively conversation may begin to develop a parched, slightly sore throat. But if the conversation is sufficiently rewarding, the speaker may not desire relief for her throat. In that case, she does not, in Brady's terms, *mind* the unpleasant sensation.[4]

If we did not mind grief's pains, then perhaps there is no paradox of grief. For, while the pains of grief are genuine, they would not be pains that we desire not occur. They would not be pains that we suffer, in Brady's terms. But then, whatever goods grief might afford us (self-knowledge or otherwise) do not stand in tension with the pains of grief. Those pains do not matter to us in such a way that there is any paradox in need of resolution.

The trouble with Brady's proposal is that, as he himself acknowledges, we *do* mind the pains of grief as we undergo them.[5] The sorrow, anguish, pining, etc., associated with grief feel bad. After the fact, we may look back on grief's pains and view them as desirable or worthwhile in some manner. But in the moment, we are neither indifferent to these pains nor do we merely tolerate them. We suffer them. I argued in chapter 1 that grief is not an emotional state but a prolonged process of emotionally driven attention directed at the loss of one's relationship with the deceased. The fact that we attend to the relationship suggests an active engagement with the source of our pain. But that attentiveness is difficult to reconcile with the thought that we "bracket" grief's pains as if we do not mind them.

3. Pain as a Cost

The previous two sections addressed attempts to resolve the paradox of grief by denying that the psychological pains associated with grief are straightforwardly or purely bad. A different approach is to take the pains of grief at face value and argue that they are costs we must bear in order to enjoy the goods of grief. In this scenario, grief's pains are just as they appear to be (painful). But if grief culminates in some good (and of course, I have argued that the relevant good is substantial self-knowledge), then these pains will at least sometimes be worth their trouble in order to attain this good. And there is nothing paradoxical about bearing a cost in exchange for an equal or greater good. Consider, for instance, an inoculation for an infectious disease. The inoculation may be painful, but it will usually be rational to bear that cost in exchange for avoiding an illness that would be noticeably more painful than the inoculation itself.

But this strategy does not suffice either. For one, whenever some cost is necessary to attain some good, we should rationally prefer to minimize that cost. If some good can be attained at some lesser cost than we "paid" for that good, that provides grounds for regret. But cost minimization does not seem to apply to grief. Intuitively, there does not seem to be any linear relationship between how painful a grief episode is and how good it is for the bereaved. All other things being equal, a more psychologically painful grief episode (i.e., one that is relatively "costly" with respect to its painfulness) is not thereby worse for a bereaved person than a less painful episode. Nor is a less psychologically painful grief episode necessarily better than a more painful grief episode. This is partly because the pains we feel in the course of grieving reflect relationships with different histories, varying levels of depth and importance to us, etc. And as we emphasized in chapters 2 and 3, grief is a response to a fact about the world, and as such, it may or may not get those facts right as far as "painworthiness" goes. It is a condition of grief being good for us that the pains be fitting in kind and intensity to their object, that is, to the relationship the bereaved has lost with the deceased due to the latter's death. (More on these matters in chapter 5.) In any case, the magnitude of the pains experienced during grief is not a rough index of how good or bad the episode itself is for the sufferer.

Thus, if this appeal to the costs of pain were plausible, it would be rational to desire that grief's pains be minimized. But it is not rational. Furthermore, this appeal to cost would suggest that the very best episodes of grief would be Meursault-like, *lacking in pain altogether*. Of course, if some measure of psychological pain is intrinsic to grief experience, "painless grief" might not be grief at all. Still, it does not seem likely that a person benefits by avoiding the pains characteristic of grief. Jollimore's argument (see chapter 3) that it would be morally objectionable to help others "wipe out" their grief supports the claim that the pain of grief matters such that its absence would not be beneficial to us. Shelly Kagan agrees:

> To be sure, normally you would rather not have lost your loved one in the first place. But given that you have, is it really the case that you would prefer not to experience any grief at all? That seems wrong; when you are aware of the death of someone you love, it hardly seems better for you to be indifferent to that fact. On the contrary, it seems better for you to be *pained* by the loss.[6]

4. Drawn to Pain

The previous three strategies tried to solve the paradox of grief by showing that grief's pains are not bad, or not bad *enough*, for the paradox to arise. Either they are admixed with pleasure (as in masochism), do not rise to the level of suffering, or are emotional costs that at least sometimes are worth bearing in light of grief's benefits. Each of these strategies fails for reasons specific to each.

Yet they share a further shortcoming. They assume that because the pains of grief *feel* bad, the bereaved are therefore averse to them—that grief's pains simply *are* bad. But this is hard to square with evidence that bereaved persons are *drawn* to the pains of grief.

The Christian philosopher St. Augustine was a remarkably subtle and attentive observer of human emotion, including his own. In his *Confessions*, he describes his reaction to the death of a close friend he had known since his childhood. Augustine gives a telltale description of the disorientation common in grief. He is puzzled as to how he could be so sad. "I became a great enigma to myself," he writes, and "forever asking my soul why it was sad, and why it disquieted me sorely. And my soul knew not what to answer me."[7] And, like Jack Lewis, his grief pervades his experience of the world, "blackening" all he observes and all that he does.

> My heart was black with grief. Whatever I looked upon had the air of death. My native place was a prison-house and my home a strange unhappiness. The things we had done together became sheer torment without him.

Augustine describes his unhappiness as "strange," yet there is little doubt that he is sad and addled. When confronted with the absence of the friend—for example, when he engages in those activities he had previously enjoyed with his friend—he is tormented by reminders of the friend.

Given the torment that such confrontations effect in him, it would seem natural for Augustine to avoid such reminders as a way to avoid the ensuing pain. Yet not only does he not avoid them, he seeks out contexts that will elicit exactly this pain.

> My eyes were restless looking for him, but he was not there. I hated all places because he was not in them. . . . I had no

delight but in tears, for tears had taken the place my friend had held in the love of my heart.[8]

Augustine is "restless" in seeking out such reminders and finds "delight" only in the tears elicited by visiting places he and his friend had frequented.

So too for Jack Lewis. "At first I was very afraid of going to places where H. and I had been happy—our favourite pub, our favourite wood," he reports. But he "decided to do it at once— like sending a pilot up again as soon as possible after he's had a crash." To his surprise, it made "no difference," for Joy's absence was "no more emphatic in those places than anywhere else."[9]

Didion faces the same sense of disorientation observed by Augustine and Jack Lewis. Her grief at the death of her husband John dislocates her mentally and physically, to the point that she worries that it is rendering her crazy or deranged. "I wanted to get the tears out of the way so I could act sensibly," she reports.[10] But Didion also hopes to conjure John back into existence, to be able to engage his dead self.

Bereaved persons thus find something *desirable* about grief's pains inasmuch they may not want those pains to end and find their cessation regrettable. The mother of a child who has died in a tragic accident will almost certainly feel grief's pains intensely. But she may very much not want the pains to end.[11]

Our effort to resolve the paradox of grief is greatly complicated by the fact that grieving persons are often not averse to the pains to grief. Indeed, they sometimes actively pursue experiences they recognize as likely to prompt those pains and worry about these pains becoming unavailable to them. On its face, there may be something irrational about these tendencies. To desire such pain may appear pathological, a form of guilty or penitent self-torture. But such desires cannot be explained away as irrational. For instance, the bereaved are not ignorant about the likelihood that their "searches" for the deceased person will be painful. Admittedly, Lewis hopes that by visiting the places familiar to him and Joy, the awareness of her absence will lift. Yet in longing for painful engagement with the deceased, bereaved persons act with open eyes and vulnerable hearts. Nor should we view this behavior as indicative of some form of weakness of will, as if bereaved individuals seek out these confrontations with the deceased against their better judgment. They are acting knowingly, with the aim of doing what they know to be painful, seemingly believing that some good will come of these painful confrontations with the deceased. They act, as some contemporary philosophers might put it, in the guise of the good.[12]

That grieving persons often desire grief's pains casts further doubt on the strategies considered in sections 1–3. This behavior does not bear the telltale signs of masochism. Neither Augustine nor Lewis nor Didion find pleasure in these confrontations with the deceased. And although grieving persons desire this pain, they do not, while it occurs at least, fail to mind it, shunting it off to the periphery of their consciousness. The mother of the child killed in an accident is absorbed in her pain, and Augustine and Lewis are deeply perturbed by not "finding" those for whom they grieve in familiar locales. They suffer grief's pains. Nor do these individuals seem to view the pains of grief as a cost. For the bereaved, these pains are not like the pains of receiving an inoculation for an infectious illness. If inoculations could be rendered painless, this would presumably be a relief, since the pain involved is a pure cost, undesirable in its own right but a pain we "put up with" in order to gain the greater good of protection against illness. The pains of grief do not present themselves as pure costs to the bereaved, however. These are genuine pains, but the bereaved perceive something desirable in their own right about undergoing them.

How is it possible then for bereaved individuals to rationally desire and intentionally pursue the pains of grief, despite these pains being unabashedly painful, i.e., forms of suffering? What is behind the apparent attraction of the pains of grief? Fortunately, adequate answers to these questions will bring the resolution of the paradox of grief into fuller view.

5. Pain as an Investment in Self-Knowledge

I argued, in chapters 2 and 3, that the various emotions we undergo in the course of grief episodes disclose various facets of our relationship with the deceased, the relationship whose loss and transformation serves as the object of grief. The sadness, sorrow, and pain we feel in grief thus discloses to us the importance to us of the deceased.

Notice that this places grief's pains in a *causal* relationship to the self-knowledge which, I have argued, is the distinctive good of grief. The pain, along with the other emotions we undergo in grief such as anger, anxiety, joy, etc., contribute to making self-knowledge possible. But notice that the causal relationship here is tighter than what holds between a pure cost and the goods that result from bearing a cost. We do not submit to the pain of an inoculation because the *pain* makes possible the protection against infectious illness. The protection against the illness results not from the pain but from how the inoculation stimulates the immune system. This is why a painless inoculation would be desirable inasmuch as it would render the inoculation less costly. In the case of grief and its pains, on the other hand, the pains are more integral to the goods in question. The pain is part of *the way by which* we arrive at self-knowledge, not an incidental by-product of the causal mechanism that in fact enables self-knowledge.

Bereaved persons, I suggest, view the pains of grief as desirable because they grasp, however inchoately, that these pains are an *investment* in the good of grief. To invest in some good is to bear a cost, but it carries a connotation beyond this. To be invested is to be committed or devoted to some good or some undertaking. Investment in some good involves seeing the means to that good not just as costs to be borne, bads that one willingly suffers in the hope of attaining the good one seeks. The means are instead viewed as good because of the integral causal relationship they stand to the good we seek.

Consider, for example, someone who spends many years writing a novel that then wins a prestigious literary prize. The many years of labor needed to write the novel and win the prize are (at one level) mere costs; they involve sacrifices of time, energy, etc., that the author will experience as laborious and *costly*. Nevertheless, the labor in question is not a pure cost. The overall value or significance of writing the novel, winning the prize, and so on, is not calculated simply by subtracting the "bads" of the labor needed to write the novel and subsequently win the prize from the "goods" of completing the novel, winning the prize. Rather, completing the novel and winning the prize alter the significance of the labor needed to do so. Completing the novel and winning the prize validate or vindicate the labor, thereby increasing the author's sense of gratification with the whole enterprise. Yes, the author will be glad that the investment "paid off." But the payoff does not consist exclusively in how the labor yielded good outcomes. The payoff also includes how the labor itself becomes good in its own right due to its essential role in enabling the novel to be completed. The labor is no longer only a negative contributor to the overall value of the author's enterprise. It also functions as a positive contributor to its value insofar as it represents an investment on the author's part. The author has realized what G. E. Moore called an "organic unity," a valuable state of affairs in which the value of the whole is not a function of the sum of the value of its components considered separately.[13] In this case, the bad or costly labor becomes good due to its inextricable relationship to the good of the enterprise as a whole.

So too in the case of grief: Its pains represent, however unwittingly, the bereaved individual's investment in the possibility of attaining self-knowledge through grieving. To the extent that grief generates valuable self-knowledge, the "pains" pay off and become something more than pure costs. Bereaved people, I propose, often anticipate this possibility and so come to desire grief's pains because they represent the bereaved's investment in the goodness of grief.

This proposal may prompt the objection that bereaved individuals could only be invested in grief's pains if they are consciously committed to the larger good that those pains make possible. But probably very few are consciously committed to the goal of self-knowledge. Few bereaved persons understand their grieving in these terms or are self-consciously guided by this goal. Hence, they are not invested in grief's pains in the way I have proposed.

Recall, though, our earlier distinction (section 3.6) between an activity's aim and its purpose. There I pointed out that an activity's various components can have particular aims without them having the activity's larger purpose in view. So too in the case of grief: The aims of the various components of grieving, including the seeking out of painful confrontations with the absence of the deceased that concerns us here, need not refer to the larger purpose I have ascribed to grief, i.e., attaining self-knowledge.

Moreover, we should not assume that in every intentional human endeavor, we know what our intentions are or that every rational action is supported by a reason we already grasp as we embark on that activity. Agnes Callard has observed that even when we pursue some activity that we expect will transform our lives significantly—and note that I have suggested that successful grieving will transform our practical identities to some degree—we need not ascertain beforehand our reasons for that pursuit. "You can act rationally," according to Callard, "even if your antecedent conception of the good for the sake of which you act is not quite on target—and you know that."[14] In such cases, we anticipate that we will change so we are able to appreciate the reasons we had for that activity, even if those reasons are apparent only at the activity's end. Such is the case with grief. We grieve in expectation of a good we do not yet know. We grieve more or less instinctually. Because we are social animals whose practical identities are reliant on the existences of others, our emotional systems are "shocked" by their deaths. But the grief that manifests this shock is not an enterprise we necessarily undertake deliberately, with a well-formed and sharply bounded goal. Bereaved persons are often, unwittingly but intelligently in my view, seeking self-knowledge without understanding that they are doing so. They intuit *that* grief is worthwhile without knowing *how* it is valuable, and act in accordance with that intuition. The bereaved therefore act in the guise of the good with only a hazy understanding of that good in whose guise they act. And of course, they may "discover," that is, bring into conscious view, their purpose as the course of grief unfolds. In these respects, grief looks like an example of what Talbot Brewer has called "dialectical activity." A dialectical activity has what Brewer calls a "self-unveiling character."[15] Beginning from an opaque hint at the purpose or value of some activity, our engagement in that activity reveals and clarifies its purpose or value. We thus come to have a fuller grasp of the activity's purpose through that activity, rather than (as we commonly assume) our embarking on that activity with that grasp already in hand. In the case of grief, the value of grieving may only become apparent in the course of grief, and perhaps in some cases, not until it has effectively concluded. But our sense that there is *some* as yet unveiled good in the activity is sufficient, in my estimation, to account for why bereaved persons can be invested in, and hence desire to undergo, grief's pain despite of and in full knowledge of their painfulness: They recognize, however murkily, that the pain conduces to some broader good.

That we sometimes act with only dim understandings of our intentions reflects the larger fact that discrepancies between our explicit cognitions and our purposes are common. In the case of grief, this discrepancy is widest in a phenomenon we might call *quasi-grief*. We quasi-grieve when we respond to the death of another with one or more of the phenomenological features of grief—distress and the like—but fail to direct attention at what I have argued is grief's object, the relationship transformed by the death of the deceased. Quasi-grief can arise when grief attends to some other object or when grief fails to attend to any object at all. The latter is likely among those who seek to suppress grief by means of distraction or denial. The former is likely in the early throes of grief when the fact of another's death is a source of emotional disorientation potent enough that grief's object cannot yet come into proper view. In quasi-bereavement, grief reactions are caused by grief's object but do not have that object fully in view. This may seem a strange possibility, but it is not. The emotions directed at a given object can mimic the emotions directed at another object. In periods of emotional tumult, our self-understanding is likely to be especially susceptible to such misdirection, so that grief can actually include a phase in which our recognition of its object is halting, gradual, or incomplete.

To explain quasi-grief in slightly different terms: We may sometimes be immersed in life narratives with little apprehension of the state of that narrative. And, as our great dramatic ironists illustrate, individuals immersed in a narrative do not always have the self-awareness to fully grasp the engines that propel that narrative or lend it its significance, even when those engines are their own inner states. Ivan Ilyich initially cannot perceive how his relentless conformism leaves him, ironically, to face death alone. *Mad Men*'s Don Draper is singularly unable to ascertain how his parents' abandonment of him explains his serial philandering. Likewise, those in quasi-grief do not comprehend where they are in their own life stories.

6. Pain's "Goodness" in the Context of Grief

The idea that we often do not recognize ourselves as invested in self-knowledge does not therefore pose a worry for my claim that in desiring grief's pains, bereaved persons are acting in the light of their investment in those pains as means to the good of self-knowledge.

A second objection to this claim needs to be addressed though: If pain is essential to achieving the good of self-knowledge, it nevertheless seems irrational for bereaved persons to desire or be invested in that pain. As I have conceded, these pains, despite being desired, are still pains and presumably bad for being pains. That they are needed for us to attain self-knowledge ought not persuade us to desire them or to think them desirable. For these pains remain bad and are best thought of merely as among the costs of achieving the good of self-knowledge—necessary and indispensable costs, perhaps, but costs all the same. To be invested in them is to illogically transfer the desirability of some end to the necessary means to that end. To do so, this objection alleges, is to fetishize the pain of grief, miscategorizing it as good or desirable simply because it enables us to attain something good or desirable.

In response, this objection has traction only if we assume that the *context* in which the pains of grief are suffered—that is, the activity of grieving—has no bearing on the desirability of those pains. But the context in which some pain is experienced can matter to how it is experienced or appraised.[16]

Take, for example, the physical pains associated with strenuous exercise, such as long-distance running. Long-distance running can involve intense sensations of fatigue, shortness of breath, muscle aches. Such unpleasant sensations are more unpleasant for novice runners. But as they develop fitness, they also develop a greater appreciation for running, an appreciation that trips something like a gestalt switch with respect to these unpleasant sensations. The unpleasant sensations remain unpleasant, but they cease to serve as reasons *not to* run (or to stop running). Rather, the unpleasant sensations become integrated into the runner's understanding of the activity of running and what is valuable about it. And insofar as they are essential to that value, the pains become perceived as reasons *to* run. In contrast, the runner would almost certainly avoid similar painful sensations when they are not connected to running. The painful sensations associated with (say) moving furniture are similar in feel to the painful sensations of running. And for the runner, the painful sensations of moving furniture are out-and-out bad, costs to be minimized or avoided to the extent compatible with moving the furniture. But that is not the case for the runner with respect to running. Granted, the more experienced runner does not desire that long-distance running be as painful as possible, but she also does not desire that it be pain-free. The elimination of pain would bring in tow the elimination of many of the goods she associates with running. So, within the context of running at least, its pains become desirable to and for the runner. She utters the mantra "no pain, no gain," but not because the pain is the cost of the gain she seeks. The pain is instead an indispensable element in an activity she finds gainful.[17]

Such an example illustrates that we cannot straightforwardly infer the badness or undesirability of pain, whether the pain be physical or emotional, solely from how that pain is intrinsically or how it feels. The larger context of attitudes and activities in which pain occurs can hold sway over how the pain is conceptualized or valued.[18] This is why some painful activities are such that participants in them nevertheless find value in those pains. Aficionados of very hot chilis or pregnant woman who opt for natural childbirth, free of pain medications, are rationally choosing pain because they desire it, where that desire operates against a background of a larger activity that they believe[19] to be valuable or worthwhile. The properties of wholes do not extend to their parts, or vice versa. And in grieving, an essential part (its painfulness), while bad when viewed outside the context of grief, can become good or desirable within the whole of the grief experience. The bereaved need not be able to articulate what that good is, however, in order to rationally seek or sustain grief's pains in the expectation of realizing that good.

Grief's pains can therefore be good within the context of the good activity of grieving. Hence, in desiring the pain that comes with seeking out the deceased, Augustine, Lewis, and Didion are not acting irrationally, even if they are not in a position, based on their own evidence, to give a satisfactory accounting of what makes their desiring such pain rational. Nor are we irrational when we conclude that it would sometimes be worse for us if grief's pains were to subside or disappear altogether. Thus, to assert that grief's pains are desirable *and* painful neither confuses the goodness of an end with the goodness of a means to that end nor illicitly transmits the goodness of grief's end to a necessary means to that end. Grief's pains are a means to the good of self-knowledge, but they borrow their goodness from the activity of grief whose tacit purpose is the attainment of self-knowledge. The sufferings of grief are therefore among those surprising forms of suffering that are not bad for us and may contribute to our lives being meaningful.[20]

7. Conclusion

Let us retrace the steps we have followed to resolve the paradox of grief: Grief is in fact valuable because it provides a distinctive opportunity for self-knowledge. Moreover, while the pains of grief are genuine, they should be understood not solely as costs we bear to secure the good of self-knowledge. Rather, within the context of grieving, grief's pains can be good and desirable because they represent the bereaved individual's investment in the activity of grieving, an investment that they need not recognize as an investment in attaining self-knowledge. We thus have reasons to be grateful for the opportunity to grieve rather than reasons to avoid it on the grounds that, emotionally speaking, it feels bad.

Note that my resolution of the paradox of grief is a *philosophical* one, intended to show that the affective badness of grief is not in principle at odds with there being something valuable or worthwhile about grief. But this resolution does not entail that any *particular* grief episode is in fact good or worthwhile for the bereaved individual. Whether grieving turns out be good or bad for someone, all things considered, is a contingent fact. But that is precisely what we ought to expect from grieving—that it sometimes is, but sometimes is not, good for us. I can think of no compelling reason to think that grief is necessarily and always good (or bad) for us.

In addition, this chapter has clarified what conditions must be met in order for grief to be beneficial to us in particular cases. For one, grief will not be good for us (or at least it will not provide us what it is *especially* equipped to provide) if it does not generate self-knowledge. In those cases, grief may well prove bad for us. For unless grief yields some other good besides self-knowledge, there is no good that could compensate for the emotional suffering associated with grief. The pains of grief are a cost with no benefit in that case. Second, even if grief yields self-knowledge, it may be that the self-knowledge it yields is small or minor when compared to the emotional pain of grief. In claiming that grief's distinctive goodness is self-knowledge, I have not claimed that self-knowledge is so valuable or worthwhile that it could overcome even the most emotionally arduous or traumatic instances of grief.

This resolution of the paradox of grief addressed arguably the largest ethical issue associated with grief—its value. There remain, however, two ethical questions concerning grief: whether (and when) is grief rational, and is there a moral duty to grieve. Those are the subjects of the next two chapters.

CHAPTER FIVE

Reason in the Midst of Grieving

A central theme of this book has been qualified optimism regarding grief. Grief's pains are genuine. But as an emotionally complex activity where we attempt to fashion a new practical identity for ourselves after another person's death disrupts that practical identity, grief presents a special opportunity: It both motivates and makes possible self-knowledge, something valuable in its own right as well as for its role in making possible a happier life. And to the extent that we attain self-knowledge, the pains of grief are themselves good, worth not only enduring but even pursuing. It is true that not every instance of grief is good for the bereaved. But grief is often good enough for us to welcome it without fear.

This chapter addresses whether and how grief is rational, and it continues in the vein of qualified optimism. I aim to explain the conditions that have to be met in order for a grief episode to be rational, and I conclude that grief is *contingently* rational. In other words, grief can be rational, but is not necessarily so.

To some extent, the questions pursued in this chapter are purely philosophical. Philosophers have long venerated reason, and much of philosophy is concerned with determining which of our beliefs and attitudes are rational. But whether grief is rational should interest us for reasons unrelated to pure philosophical curiosity. As we have seen, grief is not only emotionally distressing insofar as it involves painful emotions such as sadness, guilt, or anger. Some of its distress stems from how grief can make us feel like we are losing our grip on the world and ourselves. In the midst of his grief, Jack Lewis, for example, feels alienated from the world and hardly recognizes the person he has become. But if even severe grief episodes such as Lewis's contain an element of rationality, then awareness of this fact should reassure us. We are imperfectly rational creatures, but rational creatures nevertheless. Hence, if grief reflects our rationality rather than imperiling it, then however disorienting or distressing grief itself is, grief is not a foreign invader breaching the walls of our psyches. Rather, it instantiates an aspect of ourselves—our rationality—that we value and can draw upon to understand our grief experiences. And if grief can be rational, that should give us confidence that even if we cannot avoid grief or dictate its course, we can still manage it for our own benefit.

One way in which grief could prove irrational is if it involves disordered cognition or states of mind, such as delusions. We will return to such concerns in chapter 7, when we consider whether grief, in either general or specific cases, should be classified as a mental illness. This chapter instead looks at other challenges to grief's rationality. First, we will consider two rivals to my claim that grief is contingently rational. One is that grief is *arational*, a state or condition not open to rational assessment. According to this view, asking whether a person's grief has been rational is akin to asking whether a sneeze or a hiccup is rational—a question not to be met with a "yes" or a "no," but one to be dismissed as nonsensical. The second rival view is that grief is *necessarily irrational*, that every grief episode falls short of rationality. In this case, grief is an emotional version of psychosis. After finding reasons to reject these views of grief's rationality, I defend my own view,[1] according to which an episode of grief is rational to the extent that its component attitudes and emotions accurately represent its object, which is the altered relationship the bereaved has with the deceased. A rational grief episode will thus accurately gauge the relationship in question and its significance to the deceased, both qualitatively (in terms of which attitudes or emotions the bereaved person has) and quantitatively (in terms of the intensity or duration of those attitudes or emotions).

Still, grief presents other obstacles to our rationality. This chapter concludes by considering how grief, even when rational in its own right, may make it more difficult for grieving individuals to make rational decisions on behalf of the dying or the dead.

1. Grief without Reason

Anna and Beatrice both have occasion to grieve the death of their brother Connor. Anna and Beatrice had very similar relationships with Connor. For each of them, Connor's death instigates, as I have argued, a necessary modification in their relationship to him. Connor occupied a similar place in their respective practical identities; he mattered to Anna and Beatrice in roughly the same ways. Both are of generally sound mind, and neither have beliefs regarding Connor that are irrational (for instance, both truly believe that he is deceased, etc.). But the two sisters differ in their grief: Anna grieves intensely, whereas Beatrice's grief is Meursault-like—quiet, subdued, almost imperceptible.

Given the similarities in Anna's and Beatrice's relationship with Connor, we would expect them to grieve similarly. In particular, we would expect Beatrice to grieve more as Anna does. But is it fair to account for the difference between Anna's grief and Beatrice's grief in terms of rationality—that Anna has responded rationally to Connor's death whereas Beatrice has not?

Stephen Wilkinson has argued that the differences between Anna's grief and Beatrice's is not a difference in rationality.[2] Whatever concerns we have with Beatrice's muted grief, they do not warrant the charge that she is exhibiting a "lack of rationality." We might, for instance, think Beatrice's subdued grief is lamentable because it shows bad character, is unhealthy for Beatrice, or is upsetting to Anna (and others) who grieve Connor's death. But we would not regard a failure such as Beatrice's as a "failure to be sufficiently rational," according to Wilkinson. As he sees it, this shows not that Beatrice's grief, or lack thereof, is *irrational*, but that it is "intrinsically non-rational" or arational, not properly subject to appraisal in terms of its rationality at all. But if that is correct, then we should also regard Anna's intense grief not as rational but as arational as well. She is not responding *more* rationally to Connor's death than Beatrice, on Wilkinson's view, for grief responses simply do not answer to standards of rational appraisal.

As you would expect in light of the conclusion we have reached in earlier chapters, I do not share Wilkinson's intuitions about the contrast between Anna's and Beatrice's grief responses: Beatrice's response strikes me as irrational. But the case against grief's arationality need not depend simply on intuitions that others may not share. There are, I propose, deeper reasons to be skeptical that grief is arational.

The first is that Wilkinson blurs an important distinction between a grief episode's *being* rational and whether it would be appropriate for others to *assert* that it is or *treat* a bereaved person such as Beatrice as irrational. Wilkinson states that we would be reluctant to *criticize* Beatrice for irrationality—that "non-grieving ought not to be criticized for its lack of rationality." I am inclined to agree with Wilkinson that it might be wrongheaded or counterproductive to criticize Beatrice for grieving irrationally. We do not, after all, have to act on everything we rightfully believe to be true of others, and in this case, criticizing Beatrice for her way of grieving seems impolite, judgmental, or intrusive. Yet the fact that it would be untoward to treat her as irrational does not show that she is not irrational so far as her grieving is concerned. Hence, it could well be that Beatrice's muted grief is irrational, even though we ought not criticize her on those grounds.

Second, Wilkinson does not provide a clear account of exactly what grief is. Suppose, however, that the account I have provided is correct: Grief is an emotionally driven process of attention whose object is the relationship transformed by the death of another in whom one has invested one's practical identity. Such an account helps pinpoint how reactions such as Beatrice's could be counted as irrational (and, alternatively, Anna's as rational). Assuming that Beatrice's beliefs about Connor are essentially correct and that her practical identity was invested in Connor, she may nevertheless fail to grieve because her attention is directed, whether willfully or subconsciously, elsewhere. She may be undergoing what I earlier called quasi-grief.[3] Beatrice's subdued grief has Connor's death as its cause, but her grief reactions are not the product of her attending to the fact that her relationship with Connor has changed, and will change, because of his death. Beatrice does not recognize (yet) how her relationship with Connor must now be revamped. There are a number of possible explanations for why Beatrice only quasi-grieves. For example, Beatrice may have what psychologists call an "avoidant" attachment style, a personality ambivalent about intimacy with others, attracted to independence, and anxious about commitment. Individuals with this attachment style tend also to develop an avoidant pattern in grief, where they actively avoid reminders of the deceased as a way to cope with their loss. Thanks to this avoidance, avoidant grief is more frequently delayed or prolonged than other patterns of grief.[4] But avoidance, insofar as it represents a redirection of attention, is a grief response that, on my understanding of the nature of grief, can be viewed as a rational failure. The failure in question is not that Beatrice has false or mistaken beliefs about Connor or about the facts surrounding his death. The irrationality would instead consist in not orienting her mental faculties toward those facts so as to fully engage with them emotionally. It may sound odd to call such inattention or redirected attention a kind of irrationality. But if rationality involves having correct attitudes toward some set of facts, one way to be irrational is not to direct one's attention toward those facts.[5] In Beatrice's case, her irrationality is a failure to bring Connor's death, and its consequences for her practical identity, onto her emotional radar screen so that she can begin to adapt to it.

Wilkinson's argument for the arationality of grief is another instance of philosophical theorizing about the emotions being too crude to capture the nuances of grief. Grief is an active and emotionally driven form of attention, so its rationality (or lack thereof) will depend on how the degree to which grieving takes stock of the meaning that the other's death should have for the bereaved.

2. Necessary Irrational: Desiring the Dead Still Live

The previous section gave us reason to believe that grief responses are not arational, i.e., they are susceptible to evaluation as rational or irrational. But that conclusion is compatible with grief being necessarily *irrational*.

Donald Gustafson[6] has defended the thesis that grief necessarily exhibits what he calls "strategic" irrationality. A person is strategically irrational, he explains, when they possess attitudes that are internally incoherent in that they lead to choices or actions at odds with those attitudes. In the case of grief, Gustafson argues that it necessarily involves a conflict between one of the bereaved individual's beliefs and one of their desires:

> S grieves N's death. S knows and believes that N is dead. S has feelings of loss, pain, anger, and the like, at the loss of N. And importantly, S desires that it not be the case that N is dead. . . . Note that S's belief and S's desire are incompatible. That is, a belief and a desire, had by an agent at a given time, are incompatible in this way in case the desire is unsatisfiable on the truth of the belief, or the satisfaction of the desire requires the falsity of the belief.[7]

Gustafson would presumably say that Jack Lewis's grief manifested a kind of irrationality. On the one hand, he believed that his wife Joy had died. But Jack also desired that Joy be alive. The incoherence in question is that Jack's desire can only be fulfilled if his belief is false; Joy can only be alive if his belief that she is dead is false. It is this contradiction that, according to Gustafson, explains the painfulness of grief. Unable to fulfill the intense desire that the deceased person be alive, a bereaved person experiences a sense of helplessness. We grieve, on his view, because the other's death renders him unable to effectively act in the pursuit of our ends. We grieve "just in that there is nothing which can be done!"[8]

Gustafson's argument succeeds in identifying a way in which grief is irrational in some cases. Indeed, it would be irrational for a person both to believe that the person whose death she grieves is in fact dead while also desiring that she be alive. But we should have serious doubts that his argument shows that grief is necessarily irrational.[9]

For one, that a person's attitudes are strategically rational—in Gustafson's terms, that they do not hamper a person's ability to successfully fulfill their desires—may be necessary for a person's attitudes to be rational. But strategic rationality clearly is not sufficient for a person's attitudes to be rational. This is evident when we consider how grieving individuals could "cure" themselves of the strategic irrationality Gustafson ascribes to them. A grieving person putatively has a pair of attitudes that stand in tension:

- the desire that deceased person N be alive
- the belief that N is dead

Gustafson claims that the strategic irrationality would be resolved, and the pain of grief would dissipate, if a grieving individual could modify these attitudes so the tension at issue disappears. One way to do so would be to relinquish the first, to somehow dispel the desire that N be alive. But an equally effective way would be to relinquish the second, the belief in N's death. Suppose that we could give a bereaved person a drug that induces in them the delusion that the person for whom they grieve is in fact alive. Gustafson's view entails that this delusion would represent a rational *improvement* for that person because their attitudes would no longer be strategically irrational. For their desire that N be alive has, from their deluded perspective at least, already been satisfied! Yet it is hard to conclude that this improvement in strategic rationality is an improvement in their rationality. For holding a false belief does not ordinarily make us more rational. Hence, strategic rationality is at most part of what makes grief rational. It is not enough for grief to be rational that the attitudes that constitute it fit together. They must also fit the relevant facts.

Second, while some grieving individuals have the specific beliefs and desires Gustafson proposes, there will be many exceptions. Jack Lewis represents one such exception: As we noted in section 2.9, those who believe in the afterlife grieve. But there is a respect in which they do not hold the belief that Gustafson attributes to them. As a passionate Christian, Jack Lewis presumably believed that, although Joy was deceased, she had *not* died. For, although Joy was deceased, she continued to exist in the afterlife in some resurrected conscious form. Surely, if asked "does Joy still exist?" Jack's response would have been "yes." Of course, Jack's belief in the afterlife could be false. But given his belief system, Jack *should not be grieving at all*, according to Gustafson: For, assuming that he desired that Joy still exist, this desire was in fact satisfied.

We may thus doubt whether all bereaved individuals have the belief Gustafson imputes to them. We may also doubt that they all have the desire he imputes to them. Do all bereaved individuals desire that the deceased be alive? One difficulty here is that the desire in question could take different forms. The desire that the deceased be alive could be a desire that they be alive for their own sake. But as we saw in section 3.8, grief is a coherent reaction even when the bereaved individual believes that death was a benefit to the deceased, as is probably the case in many instances of medically hastened death. Alternatively, the desire that the deceased be alive could be a desire they be alive for the bereaved's sake. But as we saw in section 1.7, grief can occur when the bereaved hated the deceased or when the bereaved viewed the deceased as disappointing, even harmful, to them. In such cases, the bereaved person likely does not desire, for their own sake, that the deceased is still alive.

Finally, Gustafson's diagnosis of the experience of grief and what renders it psychologically painful is questionable. He views grief as a state of helplessness, as a bereaved person is unable to realize her desire that the deceased be alive. Yet it does not seem plausible that the pains of grief are due to such helplessness. As he sees it, we are sorrowful in grief because we find ourselves shackled by a practical dilemma, unable to bring about a desired state of affairs. Certainly, grief may include frustration. But frustration, being stymied in the pursuit of our desires, is more akin to anger than sorrow, and what Gustafson's account omits is any link between grief's pains and *loss*. We may well desire that the deceased be alive, but our pain is more likely due to their not being alive and the implications this has for us. As I have argued, the relevant implications are the implications it has for our practical identities. Yet even if my account of what the relevant loss is turns out to be incorrect, Gustafson's account of what renders grief painful is off the mark.[10]

We thus have reason to think that grief *can* be rational; for it does not seem either arational or necessarily irrational. What properties, therefore, make for rational grieving?

3. Grieving with an Eye to the Past

The rationality of grief is not at root strategic, as Gustafson proposes, but *retrospective*, by which I mean that its rationality is measured primarily by the extent to which it accurately responds to the object that prompts the grief experience. In other words, a grief episode is rational if the various emotions and attitudes that comprise it properly reflect the significance of the bereaved person's loss of the relationship they had with the deceased.

To appreciate this view, let us compare grief to some less complicated emotional states.

Consider again our fear upon smelling smoke. What would render such an emotion rational? Fear notifies us of perceived threats to ourselves or to what we care about. To smell smoke typically suggests the presence of fire—a threat to ourselves, our property, and so on. Our recognition of smoke's relationship to fire, and the rationality of fear as a response to smelling smoke, of course depends on our having various relevant beliefs (that fire is a threat, that "where there's smoke, there's fire") and abilities (the ability to recognize the smell of smoke). But when these beliefs and abilities are in place, this fear is a rational reaction to the fact that prompts it. In this respect, such fear is *qualitatively* rational. For the fear we undergo upon smelling smoke reliably correlates with the threat that causes the smoke. The rationality of fear has a *quantitative* dimension as well. Our fear rationally tracks the magnitude or immediacy of a threat. A faint hint of smoke, for instance, should elicit concern meriting further investigation; an intense, choking smell should instead elicit a sense of alarm, triggering our "flight or fight" response. Like grief, fear draws attention to the events that prompt it. In so doing, it will tend to motivate us to gather additional evidence relevant to verifying (or invalidating) the rationality of our initial response. Our fear rationally dissipates when, say, we find that the smoke is the by-product of a neighbor's outdoor barbecue, but rationally amplifies when we find the smoke billowing from our own kitchen toaster.[11]

A similar analysis applies to other, more "positive" emotions too. Take joy. We undergo joy in response to events that non-trivially promote our well-being or concerns. As with fear, joy's rationality requires that a psychological background be in place. The joy felt at a reunion with a friend rests on our believing that we are friends, our expecting that the friend will be pleased as well, our ability to recognize the friend *as* our friend, and so on. If any of these beliefs do not hold true, joy is qualitatively *irra*-tional; we lack reasons to be joyful. And joy resembles grief in that its particular contours are sensitive to the particulars of its object. Just as the grief we feel at the death of a president differs from the grief we feel at the death of a sibling, so too does joy take on a different hue depending on its cause. The joy felt upon closing a lucrative business deal has a *qualitatively* different feel than the joy felt when our child is deservedly recognized at an awards ceremony. This is why we celebrate these joyful events with different kinds of rituals. Cigars and drinking follow the business deal, ice cream and hugs the awards ceremony. So, like fear, joy has a qualitatively rational dimension, rooted in how it reflects (or fails to reflect) what is significant to us about its object. And joy has a quantitative component as well: A person can feel too little joy at some event, too much joy, or the right amount.

These analyses of the rationality of fear and of joy allow that they can generate desires or actions that can be, in Gustafson's terms, strategically rational or irrational. But they highlight that, generally speaking, the rationality of emotions is a matter of how aptly they respond to the facts that prompt them rather than a matter of what attitudes (beliefs, desires, etc.) we form in light of our emotional responses. The rationality at issue is retrospective, that is, gauged in terms of how appropriately an emotion reflects the significance to us of the object that prompts it.

So too, I propose, in the case of grief. Grief is rational to the extent that, and because, it fits the significance of the facts that prompt it. Again, because grief's object concerns the relationship the bereaved had with the deceased, one and the same person ought to grieve different persons' deaths differently, and two different persons ought to grieve the same person's death differently. There is therefore no universal template for a grief episode being rational. Nevertheless, grief's rationality follows the same rough contours as emotions such as fear or joy: It should be qualitatively and quantitatively adequate to its object.

In the case of grief, this picture of emotional rationality is complicated by the complexity of grief itself. As we have noted, grief is more intricate and multilayered than emotions such as fear or joy, containing not only sorrow but emotions such as anxiety, guilt, anger. It tends to involve a measure of disorientation, while also prompting questioning or puzzlement to a greater degree than most other emotional states. As such, the conditions required for a specific grief episode to be rational will be more complicated than the conditions for an instance of fear or joy to be rational. Let us spell out how a rational grief episode unfolds.

To begin, we have characterized grief as a form of emotional attention, an ongoing process wherein an individual directs their mental energies toward the loss of the relationship they had with the deceased due to that death. One way—indeed, the most far-reaching way—for a grief episode to be irrational is for it to be short-circuited at the outset because the individual does not attend to the loss of the relationship at all. The Kübler-Ross model posits that "denial" is the first stage of grief. That claim is incorrect as a general matter, but it certainly can happen that a person grasps that someone in whom she had invested her practical identity has died but she avoids or suppresses her prospective grief, whether consciously or not, by directing her attention elsewhere.[12] A person might respond to the death of a loved one by throwing herself into her work or by dulling the negative emotions of grief with alcohol or drugs. In these cases, the irrationality in question rests not on features of her grief but on the fact that she has stymied grief that it is apt for her to feel.

Suppose though that a person attends to the relationship transformed by the other's death, her attention must still "pick up on" the emotions needed for her to represent that relationship adequately. At some point, her grief should lead her to begin reconstructing her practical identity on terms that reflect her changed circumstances. But we cannot build a prospective practical identity based on a relationship that our grieving does not represent accurately. For grief is a crucial source of evidence regarding the significance of the relationships that are transformed by others' deaths. Hence, a grief episode that excludes emotions that disclose how the relationship was significant to the bereaved excludes evidence relevant to the larger project of establishing a practical identity reflective of the fundamental change that the other's death wrought in that relationship. In chapter 2, I proposed that grief experiences tend to reflect or recapitulate the bereaved's relationship with the deceased. So a relationship characterized by unresolved conflict should prompt a grief episode involving, say, anger or resentment; a relationship in which the bereaved had not been forgiven for some wrong done to the deceased should prompt a grief episode involving guilt, and so on. To be rational, then, a grief episode must involve all the emotions that would serve to disclose the significance that the relationship in question has for the deceased. Not only is a grief episode that *excludes* such emotions more likely to be suppressed or "delayed," it is not qualitatively adequate to its object.

A less common way for a grief episode to be qualitatively irrational is for it to *include* emotions that, given the bereaved's relation with the deceased, do not represent the loss in question. Guilt, especially the variety known as survivor's guilt, is a particularly strong candidate for an emotion that many people evidently undergo in grief that perhaps they rationally ought not undergo. For instance, some bereaved people believe they might have saved the deceased from death, or provided the deceased with a better death (less painful, perhaps), had they been more dedicated to them. Certainly this will be true in some cases. But survivor's guilt is arguably irrational. Soldiers, for instance, may grieve their comrades in unnecessarily arduous ways because they wrongly attribute their comrades' deaths to their own cowardice, incompetence, or irresponsibility rather than the brutal luck of combat.[13] Their guilt is understandable, even laudable, in that it highlights their sense of solidarity with their dead comrades. Still, to feel guilt during the course of their grief is irrational inasmuch as it misrepresents their comrades' death as their fault and so misrepresents crucial facts about an event central to their relationship with those dead comrades.

Emotions that occur in grief episodes may initially seem qualitatively rational but turn out, upon further inspection, not to be. In the activity of grieving, a bereaved person may investigate or interrogate their own emotional responses, which (given the object of grief) amounts to investigating or interrogating their relationship with the deceased. Such investigation or interrogation may lead a bereaved person to second guess, or even reject as unwarranted, an emotion that occurs in the midst of grief. For instance, a person might reconsider the aptness of the anger he feels toward the deceased. After recalling the interactions between them that make him angry, he may remember other facts that speak against his anger. He may recall feeling dismissed by a parent as he left home for his university studies but remember that the parent was at the same time struggling with medical or economic stresses. His anger may therefore soften from the recognition that the parent had some excuse for the dismissive behavior. Another possibility is that he has misdiagnosed the anger he feels in the course of grief. He may not be angry at the parent's actions but merely at the cosmic injustice that the parent had to die. Such an example illustrates that because grieving is a dynamic process that unearths emotions and excavates information, its rationality can improve over time.

Thus, a rational grief episode is qualitatively rational only when it includes all and only the emotions that reflect the totality of the relationship that the individual had with the deceased. As with other emotional conditions, the emotions that make up a grief must be quantitatively adequate to its object as well. If it is rational for a bereaved individual to undergo anger as part of her grief episode, then that anger should reflect the magnitude of the wrong that prompts the anger. Small slights ought rationally lead to grief with modest anger, whereas grave injustices rationally merit intense anger, perhaps even fury. Likewise for anxiety, sorrow, and the other emotions characteristic of grief: Their rationality depends not only on whether they should be felt but also on the degree to which we feel them.

Grief thus derives its essential rationality from the objects it responds to, not from the attitudes causally downstream from that response, and is rational when the behaviors that constitute an individual's grieving are appropriate, both in quality and quantity, to the object of that grief. A rational grief episode will thus accurately gauge the relationship in question and its significance to the deceased.

4. Deciding for the Dying: End-of-Life Choices

Up to this point in the chapter, I have sought to make the case for grief's being, at least sometimes, a rational response to its object. It would be folly to state with any confidence how frequently we grieve rationally. Yet my hope is that the conclusion that grief is contingently rational is both true and reassuring. Grief can feel like falling apart or losing one's way. That this may nevertheless be a rational response to one's loss should provide some measure of comfort, underscoring that grief is a reflection of our rational selves rather than a threat to them.

There are, however, certain respects in which grief may prime us for making irrational choices. This section and the next identify two contexts where grieving is likely to render us susceptible to make choices that are irrational but in a sense distinct from those we have discussed so far. Grieving individuals often must make choices concerning the dying or the dead while they themselves are experiencing a kind of identity crisis that blurs the boundary between themselves and those whose deaths they grieve. As a result, they may make choices that, rationally speaking, are supposed to reflect the interests or point of view of the deceased but in fact reflect their own interests or point of view. Such choices may occur even when our grief responses are otherwise rational in the ways that I described in the previous section. Thus, because grief inhibits our ability to occupy, in a disinterested way, the point of view of those for whom we grieve, it may compromise our psychological capacity to choose on their behalf.

The first context in which grief can compromise our decision making in this way is when we are called upon to make medical choices for a dying person. Nowadays, individuals often die prolonged deaths from chronic diseases such as cancer. Together with the growing prevalence of dementia, this entails that many more dying individuals are, at different points in time, not competent to make their own medical decisions. In some cases, they will simply be unconscious. In other cases, they may be unable to understand information relevant to their medical situations or unable to communicate their feelings and judgments. When a dying patient is incompetent, the power to make decisions concerning their medical care nearly always falls to a *surrogate* or proxy that either the patient has chosen or is designated as such by law. Overwhelmingly, the surrogate is someone likely to have strong emotional ties with the dying patient: a spouse, a parent, a child, a sibling.

Throughout this book, we have taken the grief we undergo subsequent to another's death as the paradigm case of grief. However, individuals can grieve in the expectation that someone in whom they have invested their practical identity will soon die. Such *anticipatory* grief may seem odd. However, it merely reflects the human ability to make predictions about the future and form emotional reactions on that basis. A child who anticipates Christmas morning feels glee or excitement because she looks forward to treats, gifts, and merriment. A student facing a challenging exam feels anxiety prior to its administration. That we undergo emotions prior to the events that are their objects underscores that our emotions rest on our current attitudes, even when those attitudes concern events or facts in the future.[14]

Typically, surrogate medical decision makers will, thanks to the nature of their relationship with the deceased, be strongly *attached* to them. As we observed in section 1.3, attachment is a rich form of connection to a person, involving a longing to be proximate with that person, distress upon being separated from them, a sense of security in their presence, and a belief in their uniqueness and irreplaceability. Surrogate decision makers often thus find themselves in a complicated emotional milieu: They are charged with making choices for a person they likely know to be dying, a person to whom they are very likely to be attached and whose death will therefore result in distress, insecurity, and anxiety in them. At the same time, they may well be experiencing anticipatory grief.

It would be surprising if this tumultuous emotional milieu did not shape how proficiently surrogates discharge their decision-making responsibilities. After all, surrogate decisions are supposed to satisfy a standard that is difficult to satisfy even when our emotions are less in flux. In most parts of the world, surrogates are not expected to make medical decisions concerning the patient based on their own (the surrogates') values, preferences, or goals. Rather, they are asked to make the decisions that, in their best judgment, the patient himself would have made had he been competent. They are therefore to exercise *substituted judgment*, drawing on their knowledge of the patient to choose as the patient would have chosen. The rationale for this standard is that, ordinarily, patients themselves are entitled to make their own care decisions. But when they cannot, the best way to respect the autonomy of the patient is to have a presumably informed and conscientious surrogate decide as the patient would have.

We might expect that surrogates, thanks to their intimacy with, and attachment to, the patient, would be well placed to satisfy the substituted judgment standard. After all, who is better able to choose as a dying person would have chosen than that person's spouse, child, parent, who knows them well and has a long personal history with them?

Perhaps surprisingly, surrogates often fail, sometimes dramatically, to satisfy the substituted judgment standard. One large meta-study found that surrogates, regardless of their relationship to the patient (parent, spouse, etc.), are hardly better than attending physicians at knowing patients' medical preferences. In fact, they satisfy the substituted judgment standard at a rate only slightly better than chance.[15] Other studies have found that although surrogates sometimes use information gleaned from prior conversations with the patient as grounds for their surrogate medical decisions, a surprising number admit to basing such decisions on factors with a weaker relation to the patient's preferences or values. The surrogate's choices concerning the patient instead draw upon common life experiences with the patient, their own "inner sense" about the patient's preferences or values, their own religious beliefs, or what they themselves would opt for in the same situation.[16] A person's loved ones, despite their putative knowledge of the person's values and preferences, thus do not seem especially prone to choosing the forms of medical care that person would have chosen.

Why are surrogates, who usually possess the knowledge or intimacy we would naturally expect to make them reliable choosers on the patient's behalf, so poor at making such choices? No doubt one factor is sheer emotional stress.[17] One significant source of such stress is the likely conflict that surrogates in the midst of anticipatory grief face between the prerogative to choose what the patient would have chosen and their own attachment-based interests. Surrogates in anticipatory grief recognize, at least tacitly, that an individual to whom they are attached is near death, and as a result, their attachment will end (or at least change). But losing an attachment relationship—a relationship that provides seemingly irreplaceable security, companionship, and the like—is a frightening prospect. Many surrogates are likely to opt for courses of treatment that foster or prolong their attachment to the patient, even as they sincerely believe they are choosing as the dying patient would have. Surrogate decisions tend to diverge from the patient's preferences and values in predictable ways. For instance, surrogates err more often in medical choices in the very last days of the patient's life, tending to choose more aggressive paths than the patient would have chosen. Such choices make sense if surrogates are seeking to keep the patient alive and maintain their attachment on familiar terms. Surrogates, as we saw, often choose courses of treatment they themselves prefer or assume that their own preferences are congruent with the patients'. This pattern of choice is understandable if surrogates' choices reflect a yearning to sustain their attachment with the dying patient. After all, by identifying her preferences as the patient's preferences, the surrogate retains a sense of unity or presence with the patient, eliminating or slowing the widening psychological gap between them.

As I have described, grief involves a crisis in the bereaved individual's relationship with the deceased, a crisis that revolves around their attempt to establish a new practical identity in light of the death of the deceased. A surrogate grieving in anticipation of another's death is in the earliest stages of that effort. Many surrogates will not yet be psychologically prepared to live without the attachment to the dying person, and so choose treatments for the patient that enable that attachment to continue, even if only symbolically. In so doing, they are, entirely understandably, attempting to cope with the suddenly and rapidly changing terrain of their relationship with the deceased.

Nevertheless, in a moment where she is asked to exercise a kind of impartial care for another, a surrogate undergoing anticipatory grief is likely to choose in ways that diverge from the standard of substituted judgment because of her strong interest in remaining attached to the dying patient. The surrogate is thus psychologically compromised in a manner that plausibly deserves to be called "irrational": Her attention is drawn away from the evidence that she is supposed to utilize in her capacity as a surrogate—the facts about what the patient would have wanted—and toward evidence relevant to her own attachment-based interests, with the result that the latter ends up playing the predominant role in her choices. The surrogates' relationship with the patient thus turns out to be a double-edged sword: The very intimacy or familiarity with the patient that qualifies her as a surrogate also inhibits her from choosing rationally on the patient's behalf.[18]

Crucially, though, this form of irrationality can coexist with, and even be dependent upon, grief that is rational in other ways. A bereaved surrogate may indeed choose treatments that the dying patient would not have chosen because she is undergoing grief that is, in the terms described in section 5.3, retrospectively rational. Feeling fear or anguish that accurately reflects, both in kind and degree, her relationship with the dying individual, she may opt to try to extend that individual's life as a way of slowing or stanching that very fear. Thus, she fails in her putative duties to the surrogate because her grieving *is* responding rationally to the relevant facts about her relationship with the deceased. This possibility illustrates how human rationality is multifaceted, and therefore vulnerable to fracture.

5. Deciding for the Dead: Funereal and Disposition Choices

A similar challenge to our ability to decide rationally emerges *after* the death of someone prompts grief. Often, decisions regarding funeral arrangements and the dispositions of the corpse are spelled out in a person's last will and testament. This effectively takes many of the crucial decisions regarding such matters out of the hands of the deceased's surviving family and loved ones. Yet many individuals leave no express wishes, or their wishes are ambiguous or have gaps, in which case grieving loved ones will be called upon to make decisions for—and about—the dead.

As with medical choices regarding end-of-life care, choices about funerals, etc., are complex and stressful. Such choices include the nature of the funeral service; the funeral provider to be used; whether the body will buried, cremated, or donated to science; the casket, flowers, music, catering, eulogies, notices or publicity, and other accoutrements or trappings of the service; and what legal requirements apply to the handling and disposition of the body. Such choices must be made while keeping cost in mind. (In the United States, funeral costs average around $10,000.) And as with medical surrogacy, funeral and disposition choices will frequently be made in the emotional maelstrom of grief.

The identity crisis exhibited in grief complicates these decisions in several ways. For one, something like the substituted judgment standard appears to hold sway, as the bereaved are urged to "do what he/she would have wanted." But as with medical surrogacy, that plea is filtered through the bereaved's grief experience, in which they are renegotiating and reestablishing their own relationship with the deceased. While funeral industry ethics has doubtless improved significantly since Jessica Mitford's muckraking in the 1960s,[19] some common tactics in that industry may exploit the bereaved individual's susceptibility to viewing these choices as opportunities to renegotiate or reestablish their relationship with the deceased. Caleb Wilde, a funeral director and author, observes that "guilt trips" are a common sales strategy in his industry. He cites as examples statements like "I'm sure he was the best dad ever" and "You may not have been able to provide the best for your son in life, but you can give him the best in death."[20] For a bereaved person who feels they failed the deceased in life, such statements may lead them to make expensive or showy arrangements in the hope of proving their love for, or worth to, the deceased. Wilde notes that funeral directors may also foster unrealistic expectations that prey upon the bereaved person's yearning that the deceased be safeguarded from further harm or suffering: "If you buy this vault, your husband will be protected for *all eternity*." The bereaved may also feel pressure to view the funeral and burial as acts of conspicuous consumption, spending lavishly out of a fear appearing cheap or as a way to validate the perceived status of the deceased in the eyes of the wider community.[21]

In each of these instances, the bereaved is invited to see certain choices as acts within their relationship to the deceased, a relationship (we have observed) that is being revised and reconsidered at the very moment the choices are made. On top of the fact that the bereaved may spend beyond their means for the funeral and disposition of the corpse, these choices are irrational to the extent that they are not likely to achieve the relationship-based aims that motivate them. A pricy urn will not lead to the bereaved being forgiven; costly flower arrangements do not communicate love to the deceased; and no casket is impervious to the ravages of time. Making such choices as if they are signals within the bereaved's relationship with the deceased may provide temporary solace but are largely futile gestures. Such choices are irrational inasmuch as they rarely achieve the ends that bereaved individuals hope they will.

But they are also irrational in that they are made in a self-deceptive, unconscious, or opaque manner. A bereaved person who chooses a grandiose funeral because "that's what Mom would have wanted" may in fact be making that choice to convey to his mother his guilt about moving far from her or to illustrate to the larger world the importance of a woman who was marginalized or ignored. In so doing, a bereaved person is in error about the reasons that motivate him. His apparent motives, however admirable, do not match his deeper motives. This too is a species of irrationality, for a mark of rational decision making is that our deliberations reflect the reasons that ultimately motivate our decisions. Bereaved individuals, in contrast, may sometimes make decisions regarding the dead on the basis of reasons that do not reflect their actual motives.

Like medical surrogates deciding for the dying, bereaved individuals deciding about or for the dead are thus vulnerable to making choices that blur the lines between their own interests and those of the dying or the deceased. Such blurring is understandable, even forgivable. For in both instances, individuals may be grieving rationally in that their attitudes and actions reflect the significance of the relationship they had with the deceased and their efforts to integrate their new relationship with the deceased into their practical identity. The difficulties they face arise because they must also exercise *another* kind of rationality—deciding for the dying or for the dead—that can be undermined even by grief that is otherwise retrospectively rational.

6. Conclusion

Grief, I have suggested, falls within the ambit of rational assessment. Contrary to Wilkinson and to Gustafson, it can be done rationally or irrationally. But when it is irrational, not only because it involves a contradictory set of attitudes or desires.

Most fundamentally, grief can fail to measure up, qualitatively or quantitatively, to its object, that is, it can fail to accurately and comprehensively represent the bereaved's relationship with the deceased prior to the latter's death. Yet even when our grieving is rational in that way, it is subject to other threats stemming from the need to make choices for or about those whose deaths we grieve.

CHAPTER SIX

Our Duty to Grieve

The late Robert Solomon's "On Grief and Gratitude" is perhaps the best known contemporary philosophical article on grief. Solomon makes the provocative claim that we have a duty to grieve—that those who do not grieve or do not grieve sufficiently are subject to "the most severe moral censure."[1] As a "moral emotion" "woven deeply into the fabric of our moral lives," grief is not only an "*appropriate* reaction to the loss of a loved one, but also in a strong sense *obligatory*."[2] Solomon further observes that the "degree of obligation" we have to grieve tracks the nature of relationship with the deceased, such that we are morally obligated to grieve more for old friends than for recent acquaintances.[3] "The right amount of grief," Solomon states, "speaks well of a person and his or her caring about others."[4]

As indicated by the example of Meursault, the protagonist of Camus's *The Stranger*, Solomon is probably correct as a matter of social fact. Those who do not grieve are commonly perceived as morally deficient, even monstrous. But for all the insight into the ethical character of grief that Solomon's article offers, he does not advance an explicit argument for a *duty* to grieve, and it does not follow from grief's being socially sanctioned, virtuous, or even beneficial to the bereaved that there is a duty to grieve. And it is far from obvious that not grieving, or grieving inadequately, ought to elicit the shame or guilt that typically accompanies deception, breaking promises, causing harm, or other familiar moral wrongs.[5] We should therefore be alert to the possibility that our *felt sense* of a moral duty to grieve is mistaken. As Solomon observes, "social instruction has a great deal to do with the felt obligation of grief and with perhaps the feelings themselves,"[6] so perhaps we have been acculturated to believe in a duty to grieve even though we have no such duty. And absent a convincing argument for a moral duty to grieve, the possibility lingers that our moral belief in a duty to grieve is mistaken.

This chapter's task is to provide the rudiments of such an argument. As I see it, a sound argument for a duty to grieve must address two philosophical tasks.

The first is to identify grief's *moral object*, i.e., to whom the duty to grieve is owed. As we will see in sections 1 and 2, it is unlikely that other living persons or the deceased are the objects of this duty. For, while we may owe them a duty to *mourn*, we do not owe them a duty to engage in the activity of grief. This leaves a surprising candidate for the moral object of the duty to grieve, namely, the bereaved individual herself.

The second task is to identify the moral *ground* of the duty to grieve. In keeping with the conclusion of chapter 3, I shall argue that its ground is a duty to pursue self-knowledge or self-understanding, i.e., to both recognize and rationally endorse the practical identities around which our choices and actions are oriented. What renders grieving in particular a duty is that grieving represents an especially fruitful opportunity to fulfill this duty. We thus owe it to ourselves to grieve because in grieving, we practically rational agents better grasp what we are doing in the pursuit of our good. Grieving thus facilitates greater transparency in our practical lives.

1. Dutifully Grieving for the Dead and for Others

Solomon rightly observes that grief is "very specific," bound up with the "personal suffering of a serious loss." Grief is our response to the awareness that an individual whose continued existence was assumed in our practical identities no longer exists, or at least no longer exists in the same way.

As laid out in chapter 2, grieving is a complex activity that unfolds over time, one in which variegated emotions intersperse with choices or actions. The question of whether there is a duty to grieve, therefore, is the question of whether there is a duty to engage in *this* complex activity (or a duty to do so in a particular way, or perhaps with particular motivations, etc.). This implies a richer or more complicated duty than Solomon's duty "to feel" suggests.

First, let us assume that every moral duty has an *object*—that any moral duty is such that its fulfillment is owed to some individual(s). The object of a duty can be a single individual or multiple individuals. Oftentimes we are able to specify precisely who a duty's object is: one's sister, a particular friend, a group of individuals harmed by some action, and so on. Other times the duty's object cannot be specified so precisely. We may have duties to whoever holds the winning raffle ticket or to future generations of humans without having an exact specification of who answers to these descriptions. That every moral duty has an object is, in my estimation, a relatively uncontroversial assumption.[7] Let us consider in turn the most likely candidates for the individual to whom the duty to grieve is owed.

One possible object of a duty to grieve is other living people, namely, those who grieve for a specific individual. It certainly seems plausible that our general duties of beneficence or specific duties related to friendship, etc., generate a duty to comfort, console, or otherwise provide emotional support to the grieving. In those cases where we too are grieving that individual, our duties may take on a more interpersonal and symmetrical character. Siblings might owe a duty to one another to grieve their parent, co-workers a duty to grieve a fellow co-worker, ardent fans a duty to grieve an artist, and so on. Such a duty to "co-grieve" could rest on duties related to solidarity, community-building, and relationship maintenance.

The shortcoming with understanding the duty to grieve as a duty owed to living others is that this seems to overlook the self-focused nature of grief. Whatever duties we may have regarding others and *their* grief, it is possible to discharge these duties without meaningfully engaging in grief ourselves. The duties we may have regarding others and their grief are in a certain way performative,[8] duties to behave in ways that manifest certain, often socially prescribed, modes of emotional engagement or concern. These duties are thus better described as duties to mourn, i.e., as duties to participate in ritual practices with others. Historically, mourning has been governed by exacting social and conventional norms. The Victorian demands that widows withdraw from society for one year and wear black for two years now seem positively archaic. Today's mourning norms are likely more subtle and culturally diverse. The shared rituals of mourning are often manifestations of individuals' grieving processes, yet mourning can be separate from grieving, since, after all, one can engage in such actions without embarking on the self-directed emotional activity of grieving. Moreover, mourning and grieving need not correspond in duration, and may become conceptually or psychologically divorced: A person's mourning need not be representative of their grief, and vice versa. The distinction between grief and mourning explains why hiring others to mourn for (or with) us can occur but hiring others to grieve for us cannot. Mourning can be "faked" and thus can be outsourced, whilst grieving cannot.

Notice that I have not cast doubt here on the existence of a duty to mourn. I only suggest that the supposition that we have a duty to others to mourn does not entail a duty to grieve. For the primarily self-focused complex emotional activity of grieving cannot be rightfully identified with the primarily other-focused *behaviors* associated with mourning. We may owe others a duty to mourn but this neither is, nor implies, a duty to grieve.

A second possible object for a duty to grieve is the deceased themselves: Certainly, many feel as if grief is owed to the deceased—that they would be dishonoring or disrespecting the deceased by not grieving. As we saw in sections 5.4 and 5.5, grieving individuals often feel as if they owe something to the dead. Of course, the prospect that we can wrong the dead at all is itself controversial, and I cannot hope to resolve that philosophical controversy here.[9] Let us instead assume that duties to the dead are a coherent possibility and proceed to consider whether the duty to grieve is among these. There are, in my estimation, two reasons for doubt in this regard.

The first reason is that, like the notion that the object of the duty to grieve is other living individuals, the notion that the object of this duty is the dead runs afoul of the essentially inward or self-focused nature of grief. To grieve is to undergo an emotional activity prompted by another's death. Mourning, in contrast, is more outward looking. In mourning others, that is, in publicly calling attention to the deceased, we may be discharging duties we owe to them, such as the duty to sustain their memory, bolster their reputations, and so on. We may thus have duties to the dead that require various acts of commemoration, memorialization, among others. And such acts will often be components of individual grieving. But if there is a duty to perform such acts, and this duty is owed to the dead, this is still not a duty to grieve.

A second reason for doubting that the duty to grieve is owed to the dead is that it is puzzling what the moral basis for such a duty could be. On the one hand, such a duty seems largely unrelated to more familiar duties owed to the dead. One need not grieve, or grieve in any particular way, in order to discharge the provisions of a person's will, to honor promises made to them while alive, to ensure the preservation and maintenance of their gravesite. On the other hand, other ways of grounding this duty do not seem promising. Inadequately grieving does not obviously harm the deceased, threaten her rights, and so on.

The duty to grieve, again, is the duty to engage in the self-concerning emotional activity of ascertaining the proper role that one's relationship with the deceased will have in one's practical identity, given that the relationship can no longer play the precise role it played during her lifetime. Grieving may of course involve or give rise to mourning, and we sometimes grieve by way of mourning. One may memorialize the dead, protect their reputations, honor one's promises to them, etc., as part of one's grieving, and to that extent, the duty to grieve may *entail* a duty to memorialize the dead. But this does not show that the duty to grieve is owed *to them*—that the dead are wronged if we fail to grieve them or do so in some ostensibly inadequate way. Again, accepting for the sake of argument that there are duties owed to the dead, it does not seem that grieving as such is among those duties. Put differently, there may be *indirect* duties concerning the dead that can be fulfilled through grieving, but if there is a duty to grieve at all, it is not a *direct* duty owed to the dead.

2. Owing It to Yourself to Grieve

We come then to the final possible object of a duty to grieve: the bereaved individual herself. This is the best candidate for an object of this duty. The duty to grieve is a self-regarding duty or duty to oneself. A self-regarding duty is one in which the object of the duty (again, the individual to whom the duty is owed or who would be wronged by its nonfulfillment) necessarily coincides with the duty's subject, the individual bound by the duty who would be blameworthy for its not being fulfilled. When S violates S's self-regarding duties, it is S herself who is thereby wronged.

My proposal may invite puzzlement. Although many historically prominent philosophers claimed that we have duties to ourselves, few contemporary thinkers defend such a claim, and many are outright skeptical that such duties exist. Morality, many believe, is a fundamentally interpersonal phenomenon. We will have occasion to address skepticism about the very notion of duties to self in section 3.

For now, however, let us address a more specific doubt about the prospect of our having a duty to ourselves to grieve: What is the *content* of this supposed duty? And what, in particular, does this duty morally require of us?

Unsurprisingly, I view the duty to grieve as intimately tied to what is the distinctive good that grief affords us, namely, self-knowledge of the practical identities that we fashion following the death of another. The duty to grieve is a duty to pursue knowledge of our practical identities and their component elements (our values, preferences, core convictions, emotional dispositions). And because grief is a rich opportunity for such self-knowledge, and we have a duty to pursue such self-knowledge, there is therefore a duty to grieve.

So understood, the duty to grieve is what moral philosophers term an *imperfect* duty, one fulfilled not through the performance of particular actions but by having a genuine and sustained commitment to a particular end (in this case, self-knowledge). This means that the duty to grieve does not necessarily dictate to us that we make specific choices or engage in certain behaviors. Just as the duty to be charitable does not seem to entail that we must give some exact amount to some specific cause on some specific occasion, the duty to grieve is less about particular actions or choices in isolation than whether the overall pattern of our actions and choices manifests an enduring and genuine commitment to attaining the distinctive form of self-knowledge grief can foster. Thus, the duty to grieve asks that we take some, though not necessarily all, of the opportunities for self-knowledge that grief affords us. Furthermore, the specific moral demands associated with this duty will vary from grief episode to grief episode. After all, we have repeatedly noted that grief takes on different qualities depending on the relationship between the bereaved and the deceased. A person's sibling will not grieve her death as her business partner would, for example. Hence, because the avenue toward self-knowledge will vary among grief episodes, the duty to grieve (being in turn rooted in a duty of self-knowledge) will ask different things of us in different grief episodes.

That duty to grieve rests on the duty to pursue such self-knowledge does not mean that individuals can only fulfill this duty by intending to achieve self-knowledge through grieving. I would suggest that this duty is often fulfilled by bereaved persons for whom the pursuit of self-knowledge plays little if any part in their own conscious understanding of what they do as they grieve or why they do it. Part of the explanation for this is that the self-referential aspects of grief operate in the background when individuals grieve. As we saw in section 3.7, a large portion of the activity of grieving is directed at another person, i.e., the deceased. But this conceals that these thoughts about the deceased often amount to tacit self-interrogation. To wonder whether the deceased meant to leave a note found posthumously by the bereaved, or to discover that the deceased kept a copy of a particular photo that includes the bereaved, is to be asking in part about oneself and one's concerns in the guise of puzzling over actions of the deceased. So bereaved persons who fulfill their duty of self-knowledge need not do so knowingly or intentionally. Yet this does not undermine its status as a duty.

3. Letting Ourselves Down: Self-Knowledge and Self-Love

Confusion may still linger over how grieving can be a duty to self: How is it possible to grieve in such a way that one morally wrongs oneself? In what sense could our grieving (or failing to grieve) let ourselves down morally? Is failing to attain self-knowledge really morally criticizable?

To answer such questions, we can turn to the philosopher with the most thorough conception of duties to self: Immanuel Kant. For Kant, our duties to ourselves are anchored in the demand that we show respect for ourselves as rational agents. Respecting ourselves as rational agents means protecting and cultivating the mental and physical powers needed to act effectively in the pursuit of our ends. Our duties to ourselves thus include preserving our lives and physical health, not subordinating ourselves to others by becoming their slave or lackey, and cultivating our talents. Most germane to our purposes is that Kant included a duty of self-knowledge among our duties to ourselves. To my knowledge, Kant never discussed grief. But his understanding of the duty of self-knowledge can help clarify the relationship between that duty and the duty to grieve.

For Kant, self-knowledge is ethically significant in two different ways: Either it enables us to better achieve our ends or enables us to have a clearer understanding of our moral character. Kant emphasized the latter role in particular. As he saw it, self-knowledge is morally incumbent upon us because knowledge of our own moral character serves to counteract the "self-love" that disposes us to dress up our self-interested motives in more morally admirable garb. To Kant, we tend to flatter ourselves morally, finding noble rationales for our less than morally admirable conduct that conceal our true (and less noble) motives. Self-knowledge, particularly knowledge of our own moral character and motives, thus acts as a counterweight to this tendency toward moral rationalization. The Kantian command to "know (scrutinize, fathom) yourself" is the requirement to advance one's "moral perfection in relation to your duty . . . to know your heart—whether it is good or evil, whether the source of your action is pure or impure."[10] Self-knowledge, for Kant, is how we keep ourselves morally honest.

But the duty to grieve has a Kantian pedigree that Kant's own account of the duty of self-knowledge overlooks. In the case of grief, the self-knowledge it generates is primarily knowledge of our own good, that is, of the ends that constitute our practical identities, rather than knowledge of how to realize our ends or knowledge of our moral character. Grief affords us an opportunity to re-examine our ends after another's death has shone a spotlight on how dependent our practical identities are on the existence of others. Grief disrupts, even upends, our practical identities, rendering them to varying degrees foreign to ourselves. At its best, grief renders our practical identities familiar to us again by prompting us to renovate them in light of the other's death. Having incorporated a revised relationship with the deceased into the practical identity that guides our day-to-day activities and choices, we come to know what living well by our own lights consists in, and we can be rationally satisfied that we are pursuing what is in fact our good.

I proposed in section 3.10 that self-love and self-knowledge are intertwined: Self-love is the condition wherein we care about ourselves for our own sake. In order for that self-love to seem warranted, and for us to show ourselves the kind of respect we are owed, we must grasp who we are, i.e., what matters to us. Love of someone one does not know, or does not care to know, is hardly love at all. Grief enables a form of self-knowledge where we can see ourselves more fully and richly. It clarifies what matters to us and so renders our ends, and our lives as a whole, more rationally transparent to us. Thus, where for Kant self-knowledge can only *counteract* self-love, self-knowledge (especially the kind grief makes available) also plays a role in *making sense* of self-love. And insofar as the root of our Kantian self-regarding duties is to make ourselves "more perfect than mere nature" has made us,[11] grief represents a crucial opportunity to rationally perfect our self-love. For, ideally, grief culminates in our knowing better what we are doing with our lives.

4. Addressing the Skeptic about Duties to Ourselves

If I have made a compelling case for a duty to grieve, grounded in turn in our duty to pursue self-knowledge, then there is at least one duty we owe to ourselves. Still, some skeptics may think that case is not convincing enough to overcome broader doubts about the very existence of duties to self, and if such doubts cannot be answered, a duty to grieve seems dubious.

A thorough case for duties to self is not feasible here.[12] Nevertheless, let us at least sketch answers to some of the main doubts that have been raised about duties to self and link those answers to the duty to grieve.

Some philosophers have rejected duties to self on the grounds that morality is concerned only with others and their interests. To posit duties to self, according to this objection, is to misunderstand morality's nature.[13]

No doubt much of morality is concerned with others. Our moral role models tend to be those with an unusually high commitment to others and a corresponding willingness to sacrifice their own interests or well-being in order to protect or serve others. But we should not be so confident that morality altogether precludes a concern with oneself. One of the positive moral developments of the last several centuries has been a growth in most people's scope of moral concern. Most now acknowledge not only that all actual human beings matter morally, regardless of factors such as race, gender, religion, sexual orientation, and the like, but also that human beings who do not yet exist (i.e., future generations) and non-human animals deserve moral consideration as well. Ironically, this expansion outward in the scope of our moral concern has coincided with the belief that the self is of no moral concern—that the self is owed, morally speaking, nothing at all. But the fact that belief in duties to self was commonplace as recently as two hundred years ago should induce a measure of humility: In our admirable efforts to care about others, have we forgotten that we stand in a morally substantial relationship to ourselves? Indeed, some morally significant choices people make seem difficult to capture in a moral vocabulary preoccupied solely with our relations with others. Liberal thinkers such as John Rawls have argued that self-respect in particular has a special place in our moral relationship to ourselves, a place so fundamental that a just society must provide all individuals with the social conditions needed to establish and maintain self-respect.[14] Other philosophers have argued that racism, sexism, or other forms of oppression can encourage individuals in oppressed groups to fail to show themselves self-respect, and therefore, treating themselves with respect is key to resisting their own oppression and that of others.[15]

That much of our moral concern should be directed outward thus does not support the hasty inference that *all* of it should be. It is possible to neglect or shortchange ourselves morally, suggesting that there are duties we owe to ourselves. As we grieve, we show ourselves that we matter. Grieving thus represents an act of self-love—and self-respect.

A second reason philosophers have been skeptical about duties to self is that their existence is hard to square with the principle that an individual owed some duty can always release the duty-bound individual from its performance. Take a promise, for example. If A promises B that he will X, then B can release A from the promise by waiving A's obligation. But if obligations can be waived by those to whom they are owed, this seems to drain duties to self of any force they may have: If at any point I can release myself at will from any duty I owe myself, then duties to self are so puny as to hardly be duties at all. Put differently, if having a duty to do X means that the individual to whom X is owed has a *right* against you that you do X, this right is not much of a right in the case of duties to self if you can simply waive it at your discretion.[16]

Some philosophers have tried to rebut this objection by arguing that duties to self are no less duties even if we can waive them.[17] I will suggest a different tack: While some duties to self can be waived, it is implausible that all of them can be—and all the more, the duty on which the duty to grieve depends, the duty to pursue self-knowledge, belongs in the category of unwaivable duties.

To see why, consider promising again: Suppose a person makes a promise to herself and thereby incurs a duty to herself to keep the promise.[18] She may later release herself from that promise and waive that duty. Note that both her promise and her releasing herself from the duty it generates are the products of her voluntary acts (making a promise and releasing oneself from it). These voluntary acts change the moral significance of particular facts: In making the promise, she changes the act in question from morally optional to morally obligatory. In releasing herself from the promise, she reverses that act's moral significance from obligatory back to optional. Our self-promisor thus seems to possess a kind of morally significant *power*, akin to a patient's power to consent to a medical intervention. Moral powers enable individuals, through their acts of will, to create, modify, or terminate moral facts. By consenting to medical treatment, a patient changes the moral status of an act (a physician's being in physical contact with her body, etc.) from morally impermissible to morally permissible.

In each of these cases, an individual exercises a discretionary power to change moral facts. But this then raises the question: If these powers enable this moral discretion, how do the powers themselves matter morally? Consider again making (and waiving) a promise to oneself. Each of these acts is, from the agent's point of view, morally *authoritative*, that is, they have the moral significances they do solely *because* she exercised her moral power to make and waive promises. Without putting too fine a point on it, her promising creates a duty in her because she makes it so, and her waiving the promise releases her from that duty because she makes it so. These powers must therefore differ in their moral significance from the moral facts they govern. They enable moral discretion, but they can only do so if the powers themselves matter in a *non*-discretionary way. Our ability to will new moral facts into existence through the exercise of these powers means that the powers themselves have moral significance that is *not* subject to our wills, i.e., that cannot be changed at our discretion by being waived. For if these powers could themselves be waived, then that would fail to explain how they can create, modify, or waive moral facts inasmuch as they would simply be one more fact of discretionary moral significance. We would be launched on a search for a still more basic power that allows us to waive *those* powers. Our powers to modify moral facts, and the rational agency of which they are part, must therefore constitute a kind of moral bedrock, able to influence moral facts without their own moral significance being rightfully subject to that same influence.[19]

Our duty to pursue self-knowledge, and as a consequence, our duty to grieve, are likely to be among the unwaivable duties we bear toward ourselves. By grieving, we position ourselves to know our practical identities, a condition valuable both because it enables us to better pursue what matters to us but also because such knowledge is an instance of self-love, that is, of bringing someone to whom we are dedicated into fuller view. In knowing ourselves, our rational agency more closely approximates an ideal for its exercise, to wit, that we act in full knowledge of our reasons for acting as we can or do.

A third source of skepticism about duties to self is that it is hard to explain our *accountability* with respect to such duties. Usually, in violating a moral duty to others, we render ourselves accountable to them, rightfully subject to criticism or blame, or in certain cases, punishment or sanction. One possibility is that our duty to grieve, as a duty we owe ourselves, renders us similarly accountable. Recall Solomon's remark that the failure to grieve invites "moral censure," more specifically "shame" for being "insensitive" or "inhuman." But if I am correct and the duty to grieve is a duty we owe ourselves, whatever accountability we have in connection with this duty must be directed to ourselves rather to others. The duty to grieve is not an enforceable duty, one that others are morally entitled to compel or encourage us to fulfill. In fact, those who would shame a person who fails in her duty to grieve are engaged in a kind of moral interloping, treating a person's duties to herself as if they are the concerns of irrelevant third parties.

Yet this still seems to leave our accountability for this duty opaque. Granted, the network of concepts by which we might hold ourselves accountable for violating self-regarding duties, including the duty to grieve, is likely to differ from the concepts deployed to hold others morally accountable for the interpersonal wrongs they commit. We are not likely to think of the violation of a self-regarding duty such as the duty to grieve in terms of harms to oneself or violations of one's own rights. Rather, the concepts at play include self-respect, disappointment, regret, and the like. But the fact that the vocabulary used in conjunction with self-regarding duties differs from that used in conjunction with other-regarding or interpersonal duties does not show that the former are not real duties. For instance, we have reasons for regret when we grieve inadequately. But regret differs from the resentment we feel when others wrong us in a crucial way: We regret our own actions but resent others. In grieving inadequately then, we let only ourselves down, and it is not improper to regret such failures and to direct blame at ourselves.

If these rebuttals to skepticism are not convincing, I would be content to have demonstrated a weaker, but still important, claim: Regardless of whether there is duty to oneself to grieve, we have strong *reasons* of a self-regarding moral nature to grieve. For grief presents us with a rare opportunity to relate to ourselves more fully, rationally, and lovingly.

5. Conclusion

Grieving can feel mandatory, even urgent. I have argued here that this sense is not mistaken. For in fact we have an imperfect duty—or short of that, a strong moral reason—to grieve, rooted in our larger duty to pursue self-knowledge. In grieving, we show both love and respect for ourselves. This conclusion provides further support for one of the claims from which the paradox of grief germinated: We have reason to welcome grief and recommend it to those about whom we care, including ourselves.

CHAPTER SEVEN

Madness and Medicine

Scratch the surface of grief, and madness—especially women's madness—often comes to the cultural forefront.

Consider Ophelia. As the fourth act of Shakespeare's *Hamlet* begins, Queen Gertrude is informed that a distraught and distracted Ophelia seeks a meeting with her. Ophelia's on-again off-again lover, Gertrude's own son Hamlet, has just unwittingly slain her father Polonious. "She speaks much of her father," the queen's attendant explains.

> says she hears
> There's tricks i' the world; and hems, and beats her heart;
> Spurns enviously at straws; speaks things in doubt,
> That carry but half sense: her speech is nothing, . . .

Hamlet's friend Horatio urges Gertrude to give Ophelia an audience, worrying that Ophelia may otherwise "strew/ Dangerous conjectures in ill-breeding minds."

Ophelia then enters, singing suggestively of an erotic encounter between a maiden and a young man that ends with a withdrawn promise of marriage. Memories of learning of her father's death intrude.

He is dead and gone, lady,
He is dead and gone;
At his head a grass-green turf,
At his heels a stone.

After portentously warning that her brother Laertes "shall know of it" too, she exits, bidding "good night, ladies . . . sweet ladies." King Claudius diagnoses Ophelia as mad from the "poison of deep grief," which "springs/All from her father's death." Ophelia returns later in the scene, singing childish gibberish ("hey nonny nonny") while distributing herbs to those assembled. She laments that "he will never come again."

Two scenes later Gertrude enters to inform Laertes of further "woe": After Ophelia left the castle, she retreated to the nearby woods and climbed a willow tree that bestrode a brook. "There with fantastic garlands did she come/Of crow-flowers, nettles, daisies, and long purples." Alas, the branch broke, and Ophelia fell "in the weeping brook, her clothes spread wide." Perhaps unexpectedly, Ophelia did not struggle in the stream. Instead,

she chanted snatches of old tunes;
As one incapable of her own distress,
Or like a creature native and indued
Unto that element: but long it could not be
Till that her garments, heavy with their drink,
Pull'd the poor wretch from her melodious lay
To muddy death.

"Alas, then, she is drown'd?" asks Laertes. "Drown'd, drown'd," answers Gertrude.

Ophelia's grief elicits sympathy from the other characters, and arguably, from Shakespeare himself. But their reactions also betoken a long-standing cultural tendency to associate grief with a specifically feminine species of madness. Ophelia's grief is wild; her expressions of grief are delivered staccato-like, interspersed with nonsense. She adopts the persona of a bohemian wood nymph, retreating from the world of reason and civilization. Ophelia's death, a near-suicide, is made to seem a natural by-product of an unnatural grief, understandable but also a reflection of her inconstant and unsteady womanly character.[1] Like Antigone before her, the bereaved Ophelia is represented as pitiable but also ominous, liable to upend social norms. Grief, particularly women's grief, is *dangerous*.

1. Can Grief Become Sickness?

Much of Western culture has thus tended to view grief with suspicion, as a threat to self-control and to social control, a threat disproportionately ascribed to women.[2] Subsequent scientific evidence indicates that the gentlemen do protest too much: Men and women often grieve differently. Men talk less and in more impersonal ways about their grief and exhibit more moodiness, but grief appears more emotionally vexatious for *men* than for women.[3] And while we may hope that we no longer "gender" grief as the ancients did, the question of whether grief is healthy or pathological—when, if at all, grief is a medical *disorder*—has persisted. Although grief is generally recognized as natural and normal, metaphors of healing pervade how we talk about grief.[4] Joan Didion has declared that a bereaved person is "in fact ill," undergoing a "transitory manic-depressive state" that we hesitate to call an illness only because "this state of mind is common and seems so natural to us."[5] Even "normal grief," Wilkinson observes, shares many features with major depression, including emotional pain and disruption of our normal ability to function.[6] Should we then "medicalize" grief, seeing it first and foremost as a disorder or disease? Is grief a species of madness?

Questions about the medical status of grief came to the forefront approximately ten years ago when a working group of mental health professionals charged with revising a prominent diagnostic manual, the American Psychiatric Association's *Diagnostic and Statistical Manual* (DSM), proposed changes to how that manual described grief. Until that point, the manual had observed that insofar as grief involves high levels of sadness, anxiety, changes in mood, appetite, routines, etc., it bears many similarities to mental disorders such as depression. Nevertheless, the manual did not classify grief as a mental disorder because it is "the normal and culturally typical response to the death of a loved one." The working group proposed the elimination of this "bereavement exclusion" in subsequent editions of *DSM*. It also put forth diagnostic standards for a proposed mental disorder specific to grief, "complicated grief disorder." While some in the mental health community supported these changes, opposition was intense, with critics claiming that these measures amounted to the out-and-out medicalization of grief. Eventually, a compromise was struck: The bereavement exclusion was removed, but no grief-specific mental disorder was introduced.[7]

Opponents of these measures presented several criticisms. One concern was the proposed criteria for complicated grief disorder, which stated that grief becomes medically worrisome when it lasts longer than two weeks. Two weeks, critics alleged, is insufficient for many people to "process" their grief and fails to take into account all of the many cultural and individual contingencies that shape grief episodes, such as gender, religious beliefs, a person's relationship to the deceased, how the person died, and so on. This particular criterion thus lacked the nuance needed to respond to grief in all its variety. But other criticisms focused less on the specifics of the proposal than on philosophical concerns about how medicalizing grief misses the centrality or value of grief to the human experience. Harvard psychiatrist and medical anthropologist Arthur Kleinman captured the gist of many of these criticisms, stating that "caution is needed" before we "turn ordinary grieving into a suitable target of therapeutic intervention." Speaking of his own wife's death, Kleinman claimed:

> My grief, like that of millions of others, signalled the loss of something truly vital in my life. This pain was part of the remembering and maybe also the remaking. It punctuated the end of a time and a form of living, and marked the transition to a new time and a different way of living. The suffering pushed me out of my ordinary day-to-day existence and called into question the meanings and values that animated our life. The cultural reframing—at once subjective and shared with others in my life-world—held moral and religious significance. What would it mean to reframe that significance as medical? For me and my family, and I intuit for many, many others such a cultural reframing would seem inappropriate or even a technological interference with what matters most in our lives.[8]

Kleinman's remarks echo much of what I have argued for in this book regarding grief's nature and importance: that grief reflects a vital loss, in particular the loss of a relationship that is transformed by another's death; that grief marks a transition between earlier and later ways of life; that it calls into question one's practical identity, especially one's commitments and habits. But should we share Kleinman's trepidations about seeing grief as clinical or pathological? Is he correct that doing so would amount to a "technological" reframing of grief that would deform something that matters deeply to us?

Questions about "medicalization" are not philosophically straightforward,[9] especially when it comes to psychiatric medicine. There is no clear consensus on when a person exhibits some set of properties that counts as a disease or disorder. This chapter will not attempt to settle these large-scale questions. I shall instead confine my focus to grief, arguing that we should largely resist efforts to medicalize it. Grief alters us physiologically and psychologically. Yet even when grief appears to satisfy the orthodox criteria for being a mental disorder, it is, for the most part, a healthy rather than a pathological response to the life events that prompt it. Furthermore, that grief usually is healthy suggests that these criteria may themselves be too inclusive, that is, they do not exclude conditions that meet the criteria but are not pathological. Grief thus stands as a counterexample to orthodox definitions of mental disorder. Finally, I consider the adverse effects that classifying grief as a mental disorder would have on our grief experience. In arguing that we ought to resist grief's medicalization, I am claiming that there is little reason to think that even those with very acute or intense grief are exhibiting symptoms of disease. To the extent that their grief reactions resemble symptoms of affective disorders such as depression, such individuals are not sick due to grief. A grieving person may be ill, and their illness inextricable from their grieving, but they are almost never *sick with grief*. In my conclusion, I offer a proposal for how grief should be understood from a medical or psychiatric point of view.

2. How Grief Indicates Good Mental Health

The case for medicalizing grief is simple enough: It frequently has properties that sufficiently resemble other conditions that are already medicalized, most notably, depression. But that fact should be weighed against other facts about grief that speak *against* its medicalization, some of which have been hinted at in earlier chapters.

Grief is our natural response to loss, and as we saw in chapter 3, our recovery from that loss is equally natural. While grief is emotionally taxing, by and large, most people survive it and return to lives of about the same quality as they had before a grief episode. Grief thus represents a bona fide human problem, but one that most of us have the resources to manage well enough. Complicated grief—grief that resolves slowly or involves persistent negative emotions—is infrequent, occurring in about one in every twenty-five cases of grief,[10] though notably higher for certain populations. This suggests that grief is not a pathology per se even if it can occasionally generate conditions serious enough to merit medical concern.

Some mental disorders, such as schizophrenia, are characterized by psychotic mental states such as delusions. To my knowledge, grief has not been found to be associated with any psychoses. This is not to say that grief does not impact our cognition at all. Grieving seems to lead to poorer memory,[11] reduced verbal fluency,[12] and faultier information processing.[13] But these deficits appear traceable, not surprisingly, to difficulties that bereaved individuals have with respect to attention[14] or mood.[15] As our earlier discussions of the nature of grief indicated, bereaved individuals are undergoing an ongoing state of emotionally intensive attention to the loss of the relationship they previously had with the deceased. That cognitive functions might suffer because they are distracted—their minds and hearts elsewhere so to speak—is to be expected.[16] The bereaved thus seem to lack their full capacity to engage with cognitive tasks rather than any prototypical incapacity to perform those tasks adequately. In any event, whatever challenges grief presents to our thinking, it does not introduce pathological deficits into our cognition. And in most cases, these deficits are modest in size and seem to affect only certain populations, or those whose grief is especially severe or "complicated." Grief thus does not seem to have a strong intrinsic link to impaired thought, perception, or reasoning.

Likewise, it would be shocking if our brains did not bear markers of grief. For as we observed earlier, grief is perhaps the greatest stressor in human life. Grief disrupts the ratios of mood-regulating neurochemicals such as dopamine and serotonin, as well as affecting the limbic system that connects nerves and neurons in the brain. This helps explain the panoply of emotions associated with grief. Grief also appears to affect the prefrontal cortex, responsible for planning, decision making, and articulating one's thoughts, and the parasympathetic system, which subconsciously regulates respiration, digestion, and sleep. Imaging studies have found that when women with prolonged grief are exposed to pictures of the deceased loved one, or to words associated with death, they undergo increased activity in a brain region association with reward, indicating a continued attachment to the deceased person.[17] In fact, there hardly seems to be any part of the brain left unaffected by grief,[18] and as a result, hardly any mental or bodily system that is wholly protected against grief. In short, the bereaved brain is a globally stressed brain, undergoing a multipronged assault on its emotional immune system. Indeed, some have likened the brain's response to grief to its response to trauma.[19]

Yet it is not clear that we should infer from these neurological findings that grief ought to be medicalized. Given that grief responds to momentous life events, we should expect that our bodies and minds will respond accordingly. Grief places great demands on our emotional immune systems, but the fact that we respond as we do signifies the underlying health of those systems. As the clinical psychologist Kay Redfield Jamison has eloquently put it,

> It has been said that grief is a kind of madness. I disagree. There is a sanity to grief, in its just proportion of emotion to cause, that madness does not have.[20]

A comparison: Fever is very often a sign of contagious disease. Yet as a response to contagious disease, fever is a desirable sign of the body's combatting the threat posed by that pathogen. Of course, fevers can become so intense that they become dangerous to health. So too, I would suggest, in the case of grief. Grief responses can pose threats to our well-being if they become too intense or difficult to navigate. We noted in chapter 1, for example, that grief sometimes leads to poor physical health, even death. Suicidal thoughts are also higher among bereaved individuals.[21] But that does not suffice to show that grief itself is pathological, any more than the fact that extreme fever shows that mild or moderate fever is pathological. To return to some earlier examples: Whose grief response is an indicator of better mental well-being, Meursault's grieflessness or Jack Lewis's ardent grief at Joy's death? Surely the latter, even if we may worry how much more grief Jack could have withstood.

That bereaved persons are largely well from emotional, cognitive, or neurological perspectives accords well with our findings from earlier chapters. Grief *can* impair decision making, especially (as I argued in chapter 5) when it comes to deciding on

behalf of the dead. But bereaved individuals do not appear globally impaired; their grief responses are usually fitting, both
quantitatively and qualitatively, to their objects, and while grief
often stresses us, it rarely breaks us. Grief is therefore generally
not a dysfunctional or irrational response to the events that
prompt it. Except in rare cases, our grief betokens good mental
health rather than disease, disorder, or pathology.

3. Functioning While Grieving

Grief seems to satisfy orthodox understandings of mental disorder despite not being such a disorder. But perhaps this fact
shows that such understandings are not sophisticated enough
to capture the truth about grief.

Works such as the *DSM* emphasize that psychological conditions count as disorders to the extent that they result in negative
emotion (anxiety, anguish, lack of pleasure, etc.) or impair our
"social, occupational, educational, or other important functioning" (in other words, our ability to go about our daily tasks and
pursuits). These two factors are no doubt good starting points
for thinking about when our psychological distress merits medical attention. All the same, grief possesses attributes that are not
easily accounted for in this understanding of mental disorder.

For one, whether a condition is a disorder requires attention
to the history of the condition and of the person whose condition it is. Examining only a "time slice" of a person's life for
whether they are undergoing negative emotions or suffering
from impaired functioning neglects the importance both of
how the person came to be in that condition and how the condition itself has unfolded. In the case of grief, grief surely does
resemble a mental disorder so long as we abstract away from the
fact that grief reflects facts about a person's history, and in

particular, the relationships in which they have invested their practical identity.[22] But of course we should *not* abstract away from that fact. Grief does not come from nowhere, after all. It is more than just a collection of "symptoms" to be managed. Grief is a response that is often rationally fitting in light of the object that causes it. A person who has suffered a great loss *ought* to experience negative emotion and disrupted functioning. The *absence*, not the presence, of such effects would be a sign of poor mental health. Moreover, grief episodes have their own histories too. As we noted in chapter 3, they are often not perfectly linear or predictable. Nevertheless, negative emotions or impaired functioning that would otherwise be a manifestation of mental illness are less pathological if, say, they occur near grief's beginnings. We should expect Jack Lewis to feel sad, lost, and lethargic in the early weeks after Joy's death. If those facts persisted for long enough, that might be cause for medical concern. But to determine whether grief is clinically significant, we must place the negative emotions and impaired functioning at issue in a wider personal and episodic history that recognizes how grief is often a critical juncture in individuals' lives.

Second, I have argued that grief represents a distinctive opportunity for substantial self-knowledge. To view mental disorder solely in terms of two kinds of detriments—negative emotions and impaired functioning—is to preclude the possibility that conditions instantiating these two detriments might be beneficial to individuals all the same. The orthodox model of mental disorder sees it as pathological because it represents a downward departure from some baseline of individual or statistical normality, a valley in a plain of well-being. But grief seems to be a valley which, if traversed, can sometimes lead to high peaks of self-knowledge, a peak wherein our practical identities have incorporated the deceased person in ways that reflect their deaths. On the orthodox model, feeling bad or functioning badly can only be misfortunes. According to this model, mental disorders are not opportunities for good, and the "good pain" that I suggested grieving individuals are drawn to suffer is simply an oxymoron. Of course, to suggest that grief presents us with an opportunity for good is to assume some account of what is good for us. And it seems like a shortcoming, rather than a strength, of orthodox understandings of mental illness that, lacking any deeper account of the good beyond feeling well and functioning adequately, they cannot even begin to capture why we might value grief. If, from a clinical perspective, grief simply *is* psychological pain and dysfunction, then all possible solutions to the paradox of grief are nonstarters. If the human good is defined in this narrow way, then grief cannot be good. I take this to demonstrate a shortcoming in orthodox understandings of mental disorder.[23]

As I see it then, even to the extent that grief involves intensely negative feelings or impaired social functioning (and I have in no way denied that it can), grief illustrates that a *DSM*-like understanding of mental disorder can be overly inclusive, threatening to classify as pathological what is in fact typically healthy, even beneficial.[24] Grief thus serves as a counterexample to existing medical understandings of mental disorder. For even when grief possesses the two necessary factors for mental disorder, it possesses other attributes that militate against its being viewed as pathological. This, in turn, indicates that these two necessary factors for mental disorder are nevertheless not sufficient.

4. Being Thrown for a Loop

A final reason for skepticism about medicalizing grief stems from Ian Hacking's observation that disease classifications are "human kinds," ways of classifying or categorizing human beings.[25] Classifying and categorizing human beings, Hacking observes, is crucially different from classifying or categorizing other kinds of things. When an immunologist classifies a pathogen as a virus, that classification has an impact on subsequent scientific inquiry and practice. It will guide research into how to treat illnesses linked to the virus, for example. Yet that classification presumably does not change the pathogen itself. When immunologists discovered in the 1980s that AIDS is caused by the human immunodeficiency virus, this greatly influenced our relationship to AIDS. But it did nothing to alter the physical or chemical properties of the virus itself. In contrast, human kinds have social meaning because they are "value-laden," incorporating judgments about what is good, desirable, proper, and so on. This entails that when an individual in authority classifies a person as, say, a sociopath, a musical prodigy, or learning disabled, that will often shape how that person is understood, including by that person herself. For a person to know that she belongs to a certain category can influence how that person thinks and acts. Human kinds can thus have what Hacking calls "looping effects": Being classified into human kind K can change the attitudes and behaviors of members of K, as well as others' attitudes and behaviors concerning K's members. This looping effect seems particularly in evidence with respect to medical classifications. When a person is classified as sick, social expectations kick in that were not present when they (or their condition) were not classified as sick. Consider, for example, the differences in how alcoholics were invited to see themselves before and after around the middle of the twentieth century. Before that point, alcoholism was widely viewed as a form of vice or weakness of will. Subsequent to that point, it was increasingly viewed as an addiction stemming from physiological factors. The stories that alcoholics tell about themselves before and after this change will likely differ. Up to that point, the alcoholic was a social deviant unable to overcome his moral failings, a person who ought to feel shame for his condition. Subsequent to alcoholism being medicalized, the alcoholic could plausibly view himself as a victim of nature, for the locus of causation for his condition shifted from his character to his biology or genetic makeup. In his own mind, and in the minds of others, he deserved treatment, not ostracism or reprobation. As an act of classifying someone into a human kind, a medical diagnosis thus tends to alter a person's self-concept. Unlike a pathogen categorized as a virus, a person categorized as an alcoholic (or a sociopath, or a musical prodigy, or learning disabled) will tend to conform to the expectations associated with the diagnosis because the diagnosis alters their self-concept.

Grief is a phenomenon that, I suggest, would be highly susceptible to Hacking's looping effects were it to be routinely viewed as a disease or disorder. We have already observed how grief is highly value-laden, often shaped by wider societal attitudes about who may grieve, what sorts of grieving are appropriate, and so on. Camus's Meursault is persecuted, as we saw, less for his ostensible crime of murder than for the absence of grief after Maman's death. Ophelia and other grieving women have long been viewed in western culture as aberrant and mad, a suspicion that concurrently serves to denigrate or marginalize men's grief. We see other examples of cultural prescriptions surrounding grief in contemporary culture. In recent years, doubts about the applicability of Kübler-Ross's five-stage denial/ anger/bargaining/depression/acceptance model have been voiced by researchers and by bereaved individuals. Yet the five-stage model has remarkable cultural staying power, and many bereaved persons have expressed frustration at grief counselors who subscribe to the model. They complain that counselors encourage them to see their grief experience as the five-stage model hypothesizes, even if the model does not fit the facts about their own grief episodes. The five-stage model has thus come to be as much prescriptive as descriptive, an account of how grief ought to unfold instead of an explanation of how it actually does.[26]

Contemporary beliefs about grief are also influenced by literary and media grief narratives. Didion's *Year of Magical Thinking* was a best-seller, as was Mitch Albom's *Tuesdays with Morrie*. Cinematic treatments of grief are ubiquitous, ranging from jungle adventures featuring dogs that can communicate with humans thanks to high-tech collars (*Up*) to quiet, intimate family dramas set in gritty coastal towns (*Manchester by the Sea*). It would be churlish of me to criticize these fictional treatments of grief. Indeed, we can learn much about grief from them. Nevertheless, grief narratives are a genre, predicated on conventions about how grief is supposed to happen. These conventions tend to include that grief is a lifelong struggle or wound; that grief leads to persistent depression or ennui; that "recovery" from grief requires talking through grief or some kind of revelatory or cathartic event. Such conventions do not acknowledge that most people "recover" from grief quickly and fully; that the negative emotions of grief tend to be intermittent rather than persistent, as in depression; that most people's grief fades rather than being resolved or vanquished by a single transformative event. That grief memoirs conforming to such conventions are popular attests to how their audiences have been led to expect depictions of grief to conform to a genre. But genres often correspond rather poorly to reality, and they come to reflect consumer tastes rooted in audiences' sometimes mistaken beliefs about the facts depicted in the genre (crime stories are not faithful representations of police work, and "Westerns" are hardly the place to look for accurate representations of the

American West). Genres thus become commercially entrenched. As a genre, contemporary grief narratives succeed because they ratify audience expectations. A grief narrative that defied those expectations—a narrative wherein (say) a person loses someone important to them, struggles psychologically for a bit, and not too long after returns to previous levels of functioning and well-being—would not only lack traditional dramatic virtues. It would likely baffle audiences, or simply fail to garner their attention at all.

The experience of grief is therefore strongly influenced by cultural *scripts*, shaped by expectations of propriety and normality. Medicalizing grief would create another such cultural script, a script likely, as Hacking's "looping effects" hypothesis predicts, to affect bereaved individuals and how they grasp their own grief. To be viewed not merely as grieving but *as grief-sick*, I propose, is likely to shape how people relate to their own grief experiences in ways that are largely detrimental to them. Under the sway, in other words, of societal expectations about how a person who is sick with grief is *supposed* to be, grieving persons will engage with their own grief in accordance with those expectations. And in so doing, they may impede their ability to leverage grief in the service of self-knowledge, the distinctive good of grief.

To see why, we must consider how understanding oneself as suffering from the *disease* of grief differs from understanding oneself as facing the *human predicament* of grief.

To view grief as an illness is to see the different affective components of grief—the sadness essential to it, along with the disorientation, anxiety, anger, joy, what have you—as symptoms of an underlying problem rather than bits of evidence that make it possible for us both to engage with the relationship with the deceased and to fashion a practical identity that reflects our altered relationship with them. If grief is an illness, then its "symptoms" inform the bereaved person about her putative illness, not about the challenge she faces insofar as she must adapt to the new realities created by the death of the person that instigated her grieving. A person operating within the mind-set that she is grief-sick is likely to see grieving as purely a malady rather than (as I have argued) a distinctive opportunity for self-knowledge. As a pathology, grief would be something to be "gotten over" or "moved past," not a condition to be built from. To view grief pathologically may thus discourage the process of reconstructing the self that, in my estimation, represents the very purpose of grieving.

Furthermore, medicalizing grief may mislead bereaved persons to view their condition as fundamentally passive, rather than as an ongoing state of activity in which their own wills and choices play a central role. They may thus view themselves solely through the lens of victimization and wait anxiously for grief's resolution or abatement.

Finally, there is the temptation that medicalizing grief will lead individuals to identify themselves with grief, in the way that those with alcoholism or other addictions are invited to identify themselves with these conditions. Note that those with addictions may refer to themselves as defined by their condition in ways that those with, say, cancer are not: There is no equivalent locution for cancer ("I am cancerous"?) to "I am an addict" or "I am an alcoholic." I have argued that grief has a critical role in our identity *formation*. Yet we should be wary about assigning grief a lasting part in our identity—to permanently place ourselves in a bin marked "grieving." Doing so may lead to stagnation in the development or resolution of grief and encourage individuals to have a morbid relationship with their own grief. Bereaved individuals under the influence of a "diagnosis" of grief are likely to describe their experiences not in their own language but in the language of clinical psychiatry, which tends to stymie individuals' ability to adapt over time.[27] The best resolution of the identity crisis associated with grief is not, therefore, to identify ourselves with our grief.

My worry, then, is that medicalizing grief will disrupt, impede, or hijack the self-inquiry and self-reconstruction that make grief ethically significant to us in the first place. Medicalization will alter the stories we tell about ourselves as grievers.[28] The grieving self who understands her condition as grief-sick or grief-stricken would likely experience grief less authentically. As Serife Tekin explains, the *DSM* approach to mental disorder neglects the self, thereby leaving

> mental disorder descriptions irreconcilable with subjective experiences, [directing] individual's attention away from her own understanding of her mental disorder to rely on what the *DSM* says. It becomes a challenge for those with mental disorders to understand their condition and its significance, severely limiting their ability to develop coping strategies.[29]

I am *not* suggesting that it is possible for us to have grief that is altogether free of cultural expectations surrounding grief. I *am* suggesting that such expectations can be more or less healthy, more or less conducive to fostering grief that is worth its costs. Medicalization would most likely generate expectations that put the goods of grief farther from our reach. For, in an effort to blunt grief's badness, medicalization would "loop back" into our self-concepts so as to deprive grief of its potential to afford us goods vital to a flourishing human life.

5. Conclusion

My conclusion that we should resist grief's medicalization thus rests on several different arguments. I do not take any one of these to be decisive on its own. Each one appeals to different considerations relevant to grief's medicalization, and opinions will vary as to which considerations are most relevant to medicalization. These arguments, while skeptical about grief's medicalization, are not intended to generalize in order to cast doubt on psychiatry as an institution, as thinkers such as Michel Foucault and Thomas Szasz have. My arguments do not deny the existence of mental disorder or the legitimacy of psychiatric medicine. Rather, they demonstrate that *grief* does not unambiguously satisfy any plausible candidate for a condition's warranting medicalization, and were we to routinely classify grief as a disease or disorder, this would likely do more harm than good. We should, then, be reluctant to give medical thought, discourse, and practice the power over our grief that it would likely acquire were grief thoroughly medicalized. Medicine can have a valuable role to play when grief *leads to* pathologies—depression, anxiety, or the like—, but pathologizing grief itself misrepresents it and may undermine our ability to exploit grief's potential for contribution to lives lived well.

What are the implications of my conclusion? Theoretically, we ought to oppose the introduction of a grief-specific mental disorder, "complicated" or "prolonged grief disorder," etc. Grief and bereavement should instead retain their status as a "V-code," a fact that clinicians and medical personnel should keep in mind when treating patients because it can affect the diagnosis, prognosis, or treatment of their disorder despite *not* being a disorder in its own right. In other words, that a person is grieving surely matters to how a mental health professional conceptualizes a patient and her treatment. But in this respect, grief is not exceptional, for there are many life circumstances that can contribute to the emergence of a mental disorder that is far from specific *to* those circumstances. A variety of different life stresses, such as drug use, divorce, or prolonged illness, appear to contribute to depression or anxiety, for example.[30] But in those cases, the individuals suffer from depression or anxiety, not from "complicated drug use disorder," "prolonged divorce disorder," or the like. Grief thus belongs alongside such stresses that can help make sense of the *sources* of mental disorder without themselves being mental disorders. Note that this does not preclude those whose grief leads to depression, anxiety, or other conditions, being eligible for medical assistance. It merely suggests that their grief itself is not the grounds or rationale for their being entitled to such assistance.

CONCLUSION

Grief Most Human

We are nearing the end of our quest for philosophical understanding of grief. We have come to understand the nature of
grief—of who we grieve for, why we grieve, and what grief is;
grief's value, and how despite its painfulness, it can nevertheless
be good for us; how grief is, far more often than not, a rational
response to its causes and not grounds for concluding that we
are thereby suffering from any psychiatric illness; and how, as
human agents capable of reflecting on ourselves and on the significance that the major events in our lives have on who we are,
we morally owe it to ourselves to grieve. And along the way, we
have seen that grief is not, as many philosophers in the ancient
world thought, a *threat* to our humanness. It is rather one of its
most prized manifestations. There is growing evidence that
non-human animals grieve.[1] Whether or not this is so, our complex brains and socially evolved natures ensure that we grieve
in ways that are likely to be far more intricate than whatever
grief animals may suffer. We human beings are distinguished in
part by our knowledge of our mortality—by knowing not
merely of death, but by knowing that we, like all creatures, *must*
die.[2] At the same time, our proclivity to form attachments with
one another make us susceptible to acute suffering when those

attachments are lost or threatened. Our grasp of mortality, along with our self-consciousness and our awareness of time's passage, make it possible for grief to consume our emotional attention, to contain an array of different emotions, and to prompt questions about our practical identities. In manifesting several of our most human traits, grief represents our human nature in full flower.

These lessons can, I hope, be reassuring or consolatory, readying us for the grief experiences yet to come while dispelling much of the mystery or puzzlement surrounding the grief experiences we have already undergone. Still, such conclusions might prompt the worry that we have put too happy a face on what is in fact one of life's most terrible experiences. A philosophically serious treatment of grief, one might think, demands dwelling on its badness, lest we trivialize or even disrespect those who grieve.

I have not argued that grief is *necessarily and always* rational, worthwhile, etc. Some grief responses compromise our rationality, and there will be some grief episodes that contain too much emotional anguish to be compensated for by whatever self-knowledge they happen to yield. A guarded optimism concerning grief seems warranted. Rather than being the indelible wound often depicted in popular discourse, grief instead represents an opportunity, a chance to sustain the relationships that matter to us in a new light and to achieve a more mature and pellucid relationship with ourselves. Grief can include despair, yes. Nevertheless, we should not despair *that* we grieve, for we would not be better off without it. "Between grief and nothing," as one of the protagonists of Jean-Luc Godard's film *Breathless* rightly said, "I take grief."[3]

I suggested earlier (in section 3.8) that grieving neither aims at letting go of, nor at holding onto, our relationships with the deceased for whom we grieve. Rather, in grieving, we should build from our past relationships with the deceased. In this respect, grief is a path toward *freedom*. The freedom in question is not the sociopolitical freedom associated with political movements. The freedom at issue is instead personal and psychological: Grief cannot free us from our past relationships, nor should it. But it can allow us to transcend the limitations of a practical identity that no longer suits us because it assumed the existence of the individual whose death we now grieve. In this respect, grief can be a catalyst for greater autonomy.

In a similar vein, grief affords us a chance to exercise *creativity*. Earlier (in section 2.3) I analogized grieving to musical improvisation. To extend this analogy: Grief hands us an emotional "score" that we have not had the precise opportunity to play before. The score itself is determined by background facts about the nature and history of the relationship we bore to the person whose death we grieve. These facts in turn rest on facts about the deceased's personal histories, our personal histories and identities, and how these entwine. We can of course try to resist playing the score altogether—to resist grieving for fear that the experience will prove too emotionally harrowing. If we play though, the score dictates much of how our grief unfolds. But even then, we exert *some* control over grief in the way that musicians exert some control when improvising. Grief, I argued earlier, is a state of attention and activity, not a passive condition we merely undergo. And just as the musician can shorten or lengthen a note, we can try to speed up particular stages of grief or slow them down. And as musicians can alter the feel of a piece by changing its key, we too can try to shift the emotional tenor of our grief. The kind of creativity involved in improvisation and in grief is thus not fundamentally a matter of being novel. Rather, grief is creative, as Julianne Chung observes, in that it involves making sense of or integrating a set of experiences unified by a common origin, in this case, in the fact that someone in whom we have invested our practical identity has died. "Instead of aiming at something new," Chung states, grief "aims at something that combines well with the situation of which it is a part."[4]

Of course, I have not suggested you should accept these philosophical conclusions on faith. The hope is that compelling reasons have been presented in their favor. Yet let me end by addressing two questions that might arise if you found my account of grief convincing and are trying to work out its implications.

The first question concerns the possibility that this philosophical theory of grief—most centrally, of what it is and why it matters—isn't *unique* to grief. In ordinary language, we often use the term "grief" broadly, to denote a wide range of different types of mental anguish. Furthermore, it is not implausible that we enter a state very akin to grief when relationship transformations are catalyzed by changes besides death. Couples divorce. Children move away from home. Businesses and institutions close. Employees change jobs. Those we care about suffer injuries or undergo physical decline. Celebrities, artists, and political leaders may face scandals. None of these events involves others' *deaths*. Yet in each of these cases, we may face a challenge akin to the challenge I have argued grief presents: Our relationships with others in whom we have invested our practical identities cannot continue as they were and need to be placed on a new footing. And just as self-knowledge and a reconstructed practical identity can emerge from the emotional trials of grief, so too can self-knowledge and a reconstructed practical identity emerge after these events. Hence, in characterizing grief in terms of how others' deaths transform our relationships with them and necessitate figuring out the place of those relationships in our subsequent practical identity, I may have inadvertently provided a credible account of many other crucial life events as well. In other words, this philosophical theory of grief is in actuality a philosophical account of *trauma* merely elaborated *through the lens of* grief.[5]

The focus of this book has obviously been on grief as a response to the deaths of others, and it has not aspired to make sense of human trauma in general. Still, I suspect that much of what is said here is consistent with, and applicable to, other "griefs" or grief-like states besides the mental states prompted by another's death. Grief at the deaths of another is likely to be our paradigm case of "grief," and so we can learn a great deal about these other forms by considering it in detail. Hence, if in the course of articulating this philosophical theory of grief, we have also made headway in our philosophical understandings of trauma in general, this is a welcome result.

All the same, the grief with which we have been concerned in this book—that caused by the deaths of others in whom we have invested our practical identities—is probably distinct from other traumas in both degree and kind, differences that justify singling it out as a phenomenon worth investigating independently.

As I mentioned earlier (in chapter 3), grief is perhaps the most stressful and emotionally taxing of life events. In many instances, it will be more traumatic than most every other kind of trauma we can suffer. Part of the reason is simply the nature of the loss involved: The death of a parent or of a sibling alters a relationship with someone that a grieving person will have known all (or nearly all) of their lives. The death of a long-term spouse alters a relationship that infused the day-to-day life of the bereaved. Compared to other attachments—to our jobs, say—the attachments we form with other people are more crucial to our practical identities. It is hardly surprising then that grief at the deaths of others will usually rank high on the list of traumas we can undergo.

A second reason grief due to another's death is often worse than other traumas is that the losses in question are *irreversible*. Divorce is traumatic, but occasionally, couples that divorce end up marrying one another again, as Elizabeth Taylor and Richard Burton famously did. A person laid off from her job may return to that same workplace or position. But the death of those whom we grieve cannot be undone or counteracted. Death means no return to the status quo ante. Its finality is likely to enhance the trauma of grief because the grieving individual ultimately has no rational choice but to acknowledge the death in question. For nothing she can do—and indeed, nothing *anyone* can do—can change the facts that cause and justify her grief. Grief thus renders unintelligible any hope for the recovery of the world as it was.

A third reason to suppose that the grief caused by others' deaths will be worse than other traumas in that the losses are *irreplaceable*. Recall Seneca's analogy between a deceased friend and a stolen tunic. According to Seneca, just as it would be foolish not to replace a stolen tunic, it is equally foolish not to "replace" a deceased friend. But Seneca's advice does not appreciate that our interpersonal relationships are unique and not easily replaceable. For instance, widows and widowers who remarry are likely to marry individuals who are in many ways similar to their previous spouses. After all, the widows and widowers will probably have very similar personalities, interests, and the like, as they did before their spouse died, and they are understandably attracted to individuals with whom they are likely to be compatible partners. But it would be folly to imagine that in doing so, they are literally trying to *replace* the earlier deceased spouse. Their new spouses will not have the same idiosyncrasies as the old, and in addition, they will be entering the widow's or widower's life at a very different time than the deceased spouse did. Those who remarry after a spouse's death are thus not trying to replace the spouse in anything other than a superficial sense. More deeply, the now deceased spouse *cannot* be replaced. In comparison, many other traumatic losses *can* be replaced, or at least mended. Individuals can relocate from communities ruined by natural disasters, find new jobs or professions, or remarry after divorce. Yet the irreplaceability of those whose deaths we grieve means that we may find ourselves at a loss as to what, if anything, might fill that gap. The answer I have defended in this book is that we recover from grief less by filling that gap than by reshaping ourselves so that the gap no longer needs filling. We alter our practical identities so that the gap is no longer a threat to our values, concerns, and goals. This is not to deny that individuals *in fact* recover from grief and live equally happy, even happier lives than they did before the death of the person in whom they had invested their practical identities. But when this occurs, it does not occur because that person has been replaced in any literal sense.

Hence, we have reasons to think that grief will exceed other traumas in degree. But grief will tend to differ from other traumas in kind as well.

We have seen that grief can involve many other emotions besides sorrow. One emotion it often involves is fear or anxiety. Such fear or anxiety can arise when we grieve someone to whom we were emotionally attached. The deaths of spouses, parents, or close friends can lead to insecurity because a "pillar" of one's day-to-day life is no longer present to provide reassurance, comfort, or support. But such fear or anxiety can also reflect a more *existential* form of insecurity. For others' deaths can remind us that virtually *all of what matters to us*—in the terms developed in this book, *our practical identities*—depends on realities that are susceptible to decay or destruction. Suppose that a person is grieving the death of a commanding, generous parental figure, someone whose steady and nurturing parenting was responsible for their sense of the world as safe or welcoming. It would not be surprising if that parental figure's death led the grieving person to ask, "if my loved one can be destroyed, what else can?" And the answer of course is, sadly, *everything*. No job, no dwelling, no ecosystem, no relationship, no government, no institution, is absolutely *impervious* to destruction or decay. We human beings thus live vulnerable lives, as all creatures do. But again, we must live with the distressing knowledge of that vulnerability. And lest we forget, the deaths of others in whom we are practically invested are there to remind us.

Grief is also likely to be distinguishable from other traumas in highlighting our *own* vulnerability. Others' deaths underscore the vulnerability of our practical identities to facts beyond ourselves. But because we grieve those in whom our identities are invested, their deaths are simulacra of our own and so serve to underscore the vulnerability of our practical identities to death itself. Unlike other losses, our own deaths deprive us not merely of some possible way of life or some particular practical identity. Rather, our own deaths seem to deprive us of the possibility of a practical identity altogether. Death forecloses possibilities for us because it forecloses on us. Grief thus presents us with the challenge of fashioning a new practical identity in the shadow of our awareness of the tenuousness and contingency of *all* our practical identities and even of the chance to have a practical identity at all. Such a recognition understand-ably prompts fear, even dread.

In these respects, grief likely differs from other traumas by inducing a crisis of greater depth or magnitude. For grief can shine a harsh light on our vulnerability and finitude.

The second question is as follows: A reader armed with our richer philosophical understanding of grief's nature and signifi-cance should be better prepared to grieve. (Or so I contend.) But could this knowledge prepare you so well that grief itself would turn out to be insignificant or superfluous? If a richer knowledge of grief's nature and significance can make grief more manageable and worthwhile, should we expect that same knowledge to inoculate us from grief altogether? That philo-sophical knowledge of grief would render grief gratuitous seems both unrealistic and undesirable.

Admittedly, a philosophical grasp of grief can (and should) alter how we grieve and perhaps diminish its worst emotional manifestations. In particular, that grasp may enable us to grapple with grief before the loss that prompts it. I discussed the phe-nomenon of anticipatory grief in chapter 5, grief that occurs prior to the anticipated death of another. A reader could certainly make use of their knowledge of grief's nature and significance ac-quired from this book during anticipatory grief, considering (for example) their relationship with the person whose death they are anticipating, the particular role that individual has come to play in their life, and the roles that individual could play in their life to come. A person in anticipatory grief could, in other words, anticipate the task of altering their practical identities in light of the other person's death. They could even do this in concert with the dying person, via conversations about the future after the latter's death. Such a conscientious approach to mortality and grief is probably very healthy, and what it illustrates is that the *timing* of the death of the person in whom our practical identities are invested is more incidental to grief and how it unfolds than we might suppose.

All the same, a philosophical grasp of grief will not render it utterly predictable or unnecessary. I have sought to provide a philosophical theory of grief that captures the nature and significance of this experience while acknowledging that the specifics of grief episodes vary dramatically. In the terms laid out in chapter 2, a theory of grief should aim to find the unity within grief's diversity. But a philosophical guide to grief cannot provide a recipe for *your* grief. Grieving is idiosyncratic and improvisational, rooted in our personal histories and our relationships with those we grieve. As Chung explains, grief asks that we

> respond to precise particularities of our situation (concerning our thoughts, feelings and overall circumstances) to create what we want to create. . . . This isn't something that can be accomplished by imposing a plan, even if we make various provisional and highly malleable "plans" on the fly as we go along.[6]

Furthermore, the good that grief is especially well equipped to provide us, self-knowledge, is elusive in a way that precludes our being able to leverage our intellectual understanding of grief in order to render it predictable or unnecessary. If the rich self-knowledge grief affords us—the knowledge of the values, commitments, and concerns that make up our practical identities—was easy to attain, then grief would itself be of much less value. But because we are not transparent to ourselves, we need grief to bring that self-knowledge within closer reach. Hence, knowledge of grief's nature and significance does not entail that we have the self-knowledge that grief promises to provide. This philosophical theory can therefore not tell you what the nature or significance of *your* grief will turn out to be.

Grief, I have emphasized, cannot be avoided. We can grieve smarter, but ultimately, we cannot outsmart grief. Nor should we wish to.

NOTES

Introduction

1. St. Augustine, Montaigne, Kierkegaard, and Wittgenstein are among them.

2. J. T. Fitzgerald, "Galen and His Treatise on Grief," *In die Skriflig* 50 (2016): a2056.

3. Scott LaBarge, "How (and Maybe Why) to Grieve Like an Ancient Philosopher," in B. Inwood (ed.), *Oxford Studies in Ancient Philosophy*, supplementary volume (Virtue and Happiness: Essays in Honour of Julia Annas) (Oxford: Oxford University Press, 2012), p. 329.

4. *Republic* 604d2, in *Plato in Twelve Volumes*, vols. 5 and 6, P. Shorey, trans. (Cambridge, MA: Harvard University Press, 1969).

5. *Republic* 387c–388a. For a thorough dissection of Plato on grief, see Emily Austin, "Plato on Grief as a Mental Disorder," *Archiv für Geschichte der Philosophie* 98 (2016): 1–20.

6. *Phaedo*, 117b–c, in *Plato in Twelve Volumes*, vol. 1, H. N. Fowler, trans. (Cambridge, MA: Harvard University Press, 1966).

7. "How (and Maybe Why) to Grieve Like an Ancient Philosopher," p. 323. LaBarge notes that Aristotle was a noteworthy exception to this overall picture.

8. Seneca, *Epistulate Morales* no. 63 ("On grief for lost friends"), R. M. Grummere, trans. (Cambridge, MA: Harvard University Press, 1917–25).

9. Spirit or vital force.

10. *Zhuangzi* 18, as translated by Paul R. Goldin in his *The Art of Chinese Philosophy* (Princeton, NJ: Princeton University Press, 2020), pp. 142–43.

11. Later in this book we will explore why grief can shock us.

12. C. S. Lewis, *A Grief Observed* (New York: Harper Collins, 2015). First publication by Faber and Faber, 1961.

13. Lewis, *A Grief Observed*, p. 3.

14. Lewis, *A Grief Observed*, p. 5.

15. Lewis, *A Grief Observed*, p. 12.

16. Lewis, *A Grief Observed*, p. 24.

17. C. S. Lewis, *Mere Christianity* (first publication 1952; Samizdat eBooks, 2014), p. 120.

18. Whether grief ever meets the condition for being a mental disorder will be investigated in chapter 7.

19. On this front, I recommend in particular the television series *Six Feet Under*.

20. We'll have occasion to consider grief memoirs and other narrative depictions of grief in chapter 7.

21. Lewis, *Mere Christianity*, p. 22.

22. See Lisa M. Shulman, *Before and After Loss: A Neurologist's Perspective on Loss, Grief, and Our Brain* (Baltimore, MD: Johns Hopkins University Press, 2018) for a discussion of the neurology and cognitive impact of grief.

Chapter 1. For Whom We Grieve

1. *World Factbook* (https://www.cia.gov/library/publications/the-world-factbook/index.html, accessed January 8, 2017).

2. In fact, the contrary seems to be true: There is something ethically deficient about someone who grieves each and every death. As we shall see later, such "universal" grief seems to indicate the lack of attachments or particularized relationships that make grief possible and that contribute to good and meaningful human lives.

3. Some cultures have developed highly specific mourning rituals associated with miscarriage. In contemporary Japan, a practice of *mizuko kuyo*, or "fetus memorial services," has developed as a ritual to recognize miscarriages, stillbirths, and aborted fetuses. The practices appear to be migrating outside Japan. See Jeff Wilson, *Mourning the Unborn Dead: A Buddhist Ritual Comes to America* (Oxford: Oxford University Press, 2008).

4. Kathryn J. Norlock, "Real (and) Imaginal Relationships with the Dead," *Journal of Value Inquiry* 51 (2017): 341–56, emphasizes how our relationships with deceased individuals often continue in an "imaginal" form, for example involving conversational dialogue with the deceased.

5. Monique Wonderly, "On Being Attached," *Philosophical Studies* 173 (2016): 223–42.

6. Christine Korsgaard, *The Sources of Normativity* (Cambridge: Cambridge University Press, 1996), p. 101.

7. Korsgaard, *The Sources of Normativity*, p. 20.

8. Matthew Ratcliffe, "Grief and Phantom Limbs: A Phenomenological Comparison," *New Yearbook for Phenomenology and Phenomenological Philosophy* 17 (2019): 75–95, explores the comparison of grief to "phantom limb," i.e., the sensation that an amputated or lost limb remains present.

9. Joan Didion, *The Year of Magical Thinking* (New York: Vintage International, 2007), pp. 188–89.

10. Lewis, *A Grief Observed*, p. 26.

11. For an exploration of the metaphysics of how such assertions as "I've lost a part of myself" could be true in the course of grief, see C. E. Garland, "Grief and Composition as Identity," *Philosophical Quarterly* 70 (2020): 464–79; https://doi.org/10.1093/pq/pqz083

12. Martha Hodes, *Mourning Lincoln* (New Haven, CT: Yale University Press, 2015).

13. Matt Ford, "How the World Mourned Lincoln," *The Atlantic* online, April 14, 2015, http://www.theatlantic.com/politics/archive/2015/04/how-the-world-mourned-lincoln/390465/, accessed January 21, 2016.

Chapter 2. What to Expect When You're Grieving

1. Philosophically minded readers may expect that investigating the nature of grief requires settling broad theoretical questions about the nature of emotions in general—whether emotions are primarily cognitive states like judgments or beliefs, states of bodily awareness, perceptions of facts in the world, etc. The position I advance concerning grief's nature is, as best as I can tell, neutral among these rival stances. I do not see that such questions need to be settled in order to understand grief's nature. I cannot argue for that claim here; I can only hope that partisans of these different theoretical stances will not detect anything in my account of grief's nature incompatible with their own theoretical commitments.

2. Ludwig Wittgenstein, *Philosophical Investigations*, G.E.M. Anscombe, trans. (Oxford: Basil Blackwell, 1958), part II, chapter 1, p. 174.

3. Wittgenstein, *Philosophical Investigations*, part II, chapter 9, p. 187.

4. Wittgenstein, *Philosophical Investigations*, part II, chapter 1, p. 174.

5. See Achim Stephan, "Moods in Layers," *Philosophia* 45 (2017): 1481–95, for an account of this kind.

6. Elisabeth Kübler-Ross, *On Death and Dying* (New York: Scribner, 1997).

7. John Bowlby, *Loss: Sadness and Depression* (New York: Basic Books, 1982).

8. Paul K. Maciejewski, Baohui Zhang, Susan D. Block, and Holly G. Prigerson, "An Empirical Examination of the Stage Theory of Grief," *Journal of the American Medical Association* 297 (2007): 716–23 (popularly known as the "Yale bereavement study"); George Bonanno, *The Other Side of Sadness: What the New Science of Bereavement Tells Us About Life After Loss* (New York: Basic Books, 2009); and Ruth Davis Konigsberg, *The Truth About Grief: The Myth of Its Five Stages and the New Science of Loss* (New York: Simon & Schuster, 2011).

9. J. William Worden, *Grief Counselling and Grief Therapy* (New York: Springer, 2009), pp. 140–42.

10. Again, I take mourning to be a way in which grieving may be manifest; but not all grieving is mourning, nor is all mourning grieving. This contrast will be examined in greater depth in chapter 6, when we take up the question of whether there is a duty to grieve.

11. Michael S. Brady, *Emotional Insight: The Epistemic Role of Emotional Experience* (Oxford: Oxford University Press, 2013).

12. Sebastian Wazl, *Structuring Mind: The Nature of Attention and How It Shapes Consciousness* (Oxford: Oxford University Press, 2017).

13. Wazl, *Structuring Mind*, p. 2.

14. Anthony Kenny, *Action, Emotion, and Will* (London: Routledge and Kegan Paul, 1963).

15. This claim is the basis for the popular comparativist or "deprivationist" account of death's badness, i.e., that death is bad for the one who dies because and to the extent that it results in their having a life with a lower overall level of well-being than they would have had if they had lived longer.

16. I take how bad death (i.e., the state or fact of being dead) is for the deceased to be distinct from how bad *dying* was for the deceased. Many grieving persons focus on the process of how dying was for the deceased. But this is not the state or fact of being dead, nor is it likely that this is the formal object of grief.

17. This is inspired by examples in Travis Timmerman, "Your Death Might Be the Worst Thing Ever to Happen to You (But Maybe You Shouldn't Care)," *Canadian Journal of Philosophy* 46 (2016): 18–37, and Kirsten Egerstrom, "Making Death Not Quite as Bad for the One Who Dies," in M. Cholbi and T. Timmerman (eds.), *Exploring the Philosophy of Death and Dying: Classical and Contemporary Perspectives* (New York: Routledge, 2020), pp. 92–100.

18. We will return to similar issues in our discussion of the rationality of grief in chapter 5.

19. *Upheavals of Thought* (Cambridge: Cambridge University Press, 2001), pp. 81–82.

20. Dan Moller, "Love and Death," *Journal of Philosophy* 104 (2007): 309–10.

21. Seneca, *Epistulae Morales* 63.

22. Norlock, "Real (and) Imaginal Relationships with the Dead."

23. That is, divest themselves emotionally from the deceased.

24. S. R. Shuchter and S. Zisook, "The Course of Normal Grief," in M. Stroebe, W. Stroebe, and R. Hansson (eds.), *Handbook of Bereavement: Theory, Practice, and Intervention* (New York: Cambridge University Press, 1993), p. 34.

25. *A Grief Observed*, p. 58

26. Though it should not be surprising that grief can often have physical "symptoms" as well, including digestive difficulty, fatigue, muscle aches.

27. See Kathryn Gin Lum, "Hell-bent," *Aeon*, July 7, 2014, https://aeon.co/essays/why-has-the-idea-of-hell-survived-so-long, accessed February 20, 2020, and Mark Strauss, "The Campaign to Eliminate Hell," *National Geographic*, May 13, 2016, https://www.nationalgeographic.com/news/2016/05/160513-theology-hell-history-christianity/, accessed February 20, 2020.

28. D. Klass, P. R. Silverman, and S. Nickman, eds., *Continuing Bonds: New Understandings of Grief*, (New York: Taylor & Francis, 1996).

Chapter 3. Finding Ourselves in Grief

1. Elisabeth Kübler-Ross, *On Death and Dying*.

2. Albert Camus, *The Stranger*, S. Gilbert, trans. (New York: Vintage, 1946), p. 1.

3. Camus, *The Stranger*, p. 60.

4. David Carroll, *Albert Camus the Algerian: Colonialism, Terrorism, Justice* (New York: Columbia University Press, 1955), p. 27.

5. T. H. Holmes and R. H. Rahe, "The Social Readjustment Rating Scale," *Journal of Psychosomatic Research* 11 (1967): 213–18, and M. A. Miller and R. H. Rahe, "Life Changes Scaling for the 1990s," *Journal of Psychosomatic Research* 43 (1997): 279–92.

6. I. M. Carey, S. M. Shah, S. DeWilde, T. Harris, C. R. Victor, and D. G. Cook, "Increased Risk of Acute Cardiovascular Events after Partner Bereavement: A Matched Cohort Study," *JAMA Internal Medicine* 174 (2014): 598–605.

7. I return to this possibility in section 3.9.

8. Stephen Darwall, *Welfare and Rational Care* (Princeton, NJ: Princeton University Press, 2002), proposes that a person's welfare (i.e., what is good for a person) consists in what others who care for that person would want for her sake.

9. Troy Jollimore, "Meaningless Happiness and Meaningful Suffering," *Southern Journal of Philosophy* 42 (2004): 342.

10. In chapter 6, we will consider the moral goods of grief in connection with the possibility that we have a moral duty to grieve.

11. Robert Solomon, "On Grief and Gratitude," in his *In Defense of Sentimentality* (Oxford: Oxford University Press, 2004), p. 4.

12. "Finding the Good in Grief: What Augustine Knew That Meursault Could Not," *Journal of the American Philosophical Association* 3 (2017): 103.

13. Didion, *Year of Magical Thinking*, p. 27.

14. Lewis, *A Grief Observed*, p. 28.

15. We shall have occasion to consider these controversies in chapter 7. For useful overviews of these controversies surrounding how to theoretically represent grief,

and pathological grief in particular, see George A. Bonanno and Stacy Kaltman, "Toward an Integrative Perspective on Bereavement," *Psychological Bulletin* 125 (1999): 760–76, and Colin Murray Parkes, "Grief: Lessons from the Past, Visions for the Future," *Psychologica Belgica* 50 (2010), especially pp. 18–22.

16. Though it should not be surprising that grief can often have physical "symptoms" as well, including digestive difficulty, fatigue, muscle aches, and so on.

17. "Love's Knowledge," in B. McLaughlin and A. Rorty (eds.), *Perspectives on Self-Deception* (Berkeley: University of California Press, 1988), p. 487.

18. "Love's Knowledge," p. 490 (emphasis added).

19. Didion, *Year of Magical Thinking*, p. 68.

20. Harry Frankfurt, *The Importance of What We Care About* (New York: Cambridge University Press, 1988), p. 83. Indeed, it is a mark of *feigned* grief that the bereaved is not eudaimonically invested in the deceased's continued existence. See Tony Milligan, "False Emotions," *Philosophy* 83 (2008): 213–30, and Jollimore, "Meaningless Happiness and Meaningful Suffering," pp. 339–40.

21. That out-and-out denial, the delusional belief that the individual is still alive, is in fact very uncommon in grief is one of the chief findings of Maciejewski et al., "An Empirical Examination of the Stage Theory of Grief."

22. Rick Anthony Furtak, *Knowing Emotions: Truthfulness and Recognition in Affective Experience* (Oxford: Oxford University Press, 2018), p. 78.

23. A central theme of Solomon's "On Grief and Gratitude" is that dismissive attitudes toward grief and an unwillingness to express gratitude are rooted in a common (but mistaken) rejection of human vulnerability and interdependence.

24. For more on how grief breaks down habitual patterns of life, see Peter Whybrow, *A Mood Apart* (London: Picador, 1997); Kym Maclaren, "Emotional Clichés and Authentic Passions: A Phenomenological Revision of a Cognitive Theory of Emotion," *Phenomenology and the Cognitive Sciences* 10 (2011): 62–63; and Matthew Ratcliffe, "Relating to the Dead: Social Cognition and the Phenomenology of Grief," in Thomas Szanto and Dermot Moran (eds.), *Phenomenology of Sociality: Discovering the 'We,'* (New York: Routledge, 2016), pp. 202–15.

25. *Not* grieving someone's death is also a catalyst for self-knowledge, on my view; it indicates that one no longer does, and perhaps never did, have an identity-constituting relationship with the deceased individual. We may thus be surprised by our failure to grieve because we had too easily assumed that such a relationship existed.

26. Stephen Mulhall, "Can There Be an Epistemology of Moods?" *Royal Institute of Philosophy Supplement* 41 (1996): 192.

27. "The Dual Process Model of Coping with Bereavement: A Decade On," *OMEGA* 61 (2010): 277.

28. Ester Shapiro, *Grief as a Family Process: A Developmental Approach to Clinical Practice* (New York: Guilford, 1994); Tony Walter, "A New Model of Grief: Bereavement and Biography," *Mortality* 1 (1996): 7–25; and S. M. Andersen and S. Chen, "The Relational Self: An Interpersonal Social Cognitive Theory," *Psychological Review* 109 (2002): 619–45.

29. Ami Harbin, *Disorientation and Moral Life* (Oxford: Oxford University Press, 2016), p. 2.

30. Owen Earshaw, "Disorientation and Cognitive Enquiry," in L. Candiotto (ed.), *The Value of Emotions for Knowledge* (London: Palgrave MacMillan, 2019), p. 180.

31. Colin Parkes, *Bereavement: Studies of Grief in Adult Life* (London: Penguin, 1996), p. 90.

32. Matthew Ratcliffe develops themes from the phenomenology of Maurice Merleau-Ponty to suggest that grief is experienced as an "interplay of presence, absence, and indeterminacy that pervades the world of the bereaved" ("Towards a Phenomenology of Grief: Insights from Merleau-Ponty," *European Journal of Philosophy* 2019, DOI: 10.1111/ejop.12513). On the theme of grief intertwining past experience of the deceased as present and current experience of the deceased as absent, see Thomas Fuchs, "Presence in Absence: The Ambiguous Phenomenology of Grief," *Phenomenology and the Cognitive Sciences* 17 (2018): 43–63.

33. "Love and Death," in J. Deigh (ed.), *On Emotions: Philosophical Essays* (Oxford: Oxford University Press, 2013), p. 173.

34. James Morey, *Living with Grief and Mourning* (Manchester: Manchester University Press, 1995), and Colin Parkes and Holly Prigerson, *Bereavement: Studies of Grief in Adult Life*, 4th ed. (New York: Routledge, 2010).

35. Lewis, *A Grief Observed*, p. 25. See also Ratcliffe, "Grief and Phantom Limbs: A Phenomenological Comparison," and Ratcliffe, "Toward a Phenomenology of Grief," pp. 2–3.

36. Lewis, *A Grief Observed*, p. 5.

37. Lewis, *A Grief Observed*, p. 17.

38. Lewis, *A Grief Observed*, p. 25.

39. *Self-Knowledge for Humans* (Oxford: Oxford University Press, 2014), p. 10. Thomas Attig defends a similar claim, arguing that grief involves "relearning" our selves, the world, and our relationship with the deceased; *How We Grieve: Relearning the World*, revised edition (Oxford: Oxford University Press, 2011).

40. Solomon, "On Grief and Gratitude."

41. Brady, *Emotional Insight*, p. 154.

42. Furtak, *Knowing Emotions*, p. 20.

43. Norlock, "Real (and) Imaginal Relationships with the Dead."

44. Ratcliffe, "Relating to the Dead: Social Cognition and the Phenomenology of Grief."

45. Ratcliffe also proposes that this second-personal interaction fosters appreciation of how death has rendered *their* world unintelligible to them ("Relating to the Dead," p. 211).

46. See Alexis Elder, "Conversation from Beyond the Grave? A Neo-Confucian Ethics of Chatbots of the Dead," *Journal of Applied Philosophy* 2019, https://doi.org/10.1111/japp.12369, and Patrick Stokes, "Ghosts in the Machine: Do the Dead Live on in Facebook?" *Philosophy and Technology* 25 (2012): 363–79.

47. Furtak, *Knowing Emotions*, p. 36. See also Moller, "Love and the Rationality of Grief," in C. Grau and A. Smuts (eds.), *Oxford Handbook of the Philosophy of Love* (Oxford: Oxford University Press, 2017), p. 11. DOI: 10.1093/oxfordhb/9780199395729.013.35

48. Alexandra Zinck, "Self-referential Emotions," *Consciousness and Cognition* 17 (2008): 496–505.

49. Chai M. Tyng et al., "The Influences of Emotion on Learning and Memory," *Frontiers in Psychology* 8 (2017):1454. DOI:10.3389/fpsyg.2017.01454

50. Sigmund Freud, in "Mourning and Melancholia," *Internationale Zeitschrift für Ärztliche Psychoanalyse [International Journal for Medical Psychoanalysis]* 4 (1917): 288–301.

51. See Bonanno, *The Other Side of Sadness*, and Konigsberg, *The Truth About Grief*.

52. Walter, "A New Model of Grief: Bereavement and Biography."

53. A. Futterman, J. Peterson, and M. Gilewski, "The Effects of Late-Life Spousal Bereavement Over a 30-Month Interval," *Psychology and Aging* 6 (1991): 434–41; S. Zisook et al., "The Many Faces of Depression Following Spousal Bereavement," *Journal of Affective Disorders* 45 (1997): 85–94; George Bonanno et al., "Resilience to Loss and Chronic Grief: A Prospective Study from Preloss to 18-Months Postloss," *Journal of Personality and Social Psychology* 83 (2002): 1150–64; Bonanno al., "Grief Processing and Deliberate Grief Avoidance: A Prospective Comparison of Bereaved Spouses and Parents in the United States and the People's Republic of China," *Journal of Consulting and Clinical Psychology* 73 (2005): 86–98; Bonanno et al., "Resilience to Loss in Bereaved Spouses, Bereaved Parents, and Bereaved Gay Men," *Journal of Personality and Social Psychology* 88 (2005): 827–43. For overviews of this research, see M. Luhmann et al., "Subjective Well-Being and Adaptation to Life Events: A Meta-Analysis," *Journal of Personality and Social Psychology* 102 (2012): 592–615, and Bonanno, *The Other Side of Sadness*, chapter 4.

54. Moller, "Love and Death."

55. Ryan Preston-Roedder and Erica Preston-Roedder, "Grief and Recovery," in A. Gottlib (ed.), *The Moral Psychology of Sadness* (London: Rowman & Littlefield, 2017), pp. 93–116.

56. Aaron Smuts, "Love and Death: The Problem of Resilience," in Michael Cholbi (ed.), *Immortality and the Philosophy of Death* (London: Rowman & Littlefield, 2015), pp. 173–88.

57. Lewis, *A Grief Observed*, p. 17.

58. Lewis, *A Grief Observed*, pp. 1, 8.

59. Daniel Russell, *Happiness for Humans* (Oxford: Oxford University Press, 2012), pp. 224–27.

60. Moller, "Love and the Rationality of Grief," p. 8.

61. Moller, "Love and Death," p. 311. See also "Love and the Rationality of Grief," pp. 2–3.

62. Part of my disagreement with Moller stems from an underlying disagreement about what the object of grief is. He believes that we grieve for the loss of the person ("Love and the Rationality of Grief," p. 10), whereas I believe we grieve for the loss of the relationship as it was. Again, that grief's object concerns the loss of the relationship as it was explains a wide array of facts about grief: that grieving is selective; that the course of grieving varies both for and among individuals, depending on the nature of their relationship with the deceased; that the death of the other causes feelings of disorientation or loss of self; that we grieve for individuals to whom we are not emotionally intimate; etc. Moller's position that the object is the loss of the person, in contrast, can account for the fact *that* we grieve for those with whom we had a relationship. But it says little about *which* relationships make grief possible, *how* we grieve, *when* we grieve (for how long or in what pattern, etc.), and ultimately *why* we grieve. For further elaboration of this critique of Moller and whether we should ever regret how we grieve, see my "Regret, Resilience, and the Nature of Grief," *Journal of Moral Philosophy* 16 (2019): 486–508.

63. The argument that follows is greatly influenced by Jordan MacKenzie, "Knowing Yourself and Being Worth Knowing," *Journal of the American Philosophical Association* 4 (2018): 243–61.

64. I have argued elsewhere that suicidal ideation can be viewed in terms of an individual having lost her capacity for self-love. See "Suicide Intervention and Nonideal Kantian Theory," *Journal of Applied Philosophy* 19 (2002): 245–59; and "A Kantian Defense of Prudential Suicide," *Journal of Moral Philosophy* 7 (2010): 489–515.

65. The notion that romantic love in particular involves a special form of seeing and identifying with the loved person is a prominent theme in Troy Jollimore, *Love's Vision* (Princeton, NJ: Princeton University Press, 2011).

Chapter 4. Making Good on the Pain

1. Aristotle, *Rhetoric*, 1378a.

2. Hume, "Of Tragedy."

3. Colin Klein, "The Penumbral Theory of Masochistic Pleasure," *Review of Philosophy and Psychology* 5 (2014): 41–55.

4. Michael Brady, *Suffering and Virtue* (Oxford: Oxford University Press, 2018), pp. 26–32.

5. Brady, *Suffering and Virtue*, p. 17.

6. "An Introduction to Ill-Being," in M. Timmons (ed.), *Oxford Studies in Normative Ethics*, vol. 4 (Oxford: Oxford University Press, 2014), p. 267.

7. St. Augustine, *Confessions*, F. Sheed, trans., Michael P. Foley, ed. (Indianapolis, IN: Hackett, 2006), 4.4.59. [Original composition AD 397–400.]

8. St. Augustine, *Confessions*, 4.4.59–60.

9. Lewis, *A Grief Observed*, p. 5.

10. Dideon, *Year of Magical Thinking*, p. 52.

11. Antti Kauppinen, "The World According to Suffering," in Michael Brady, David Bain, and Jennifer Corns (eds.), *The Philosophy of Suffering* (London: Routledge, 2019), pp. 2–20.

12. Joseph Raz, "On the Guise of the Good," in Sergio Tenenbaum (ed.), *Desire, Practical Reason, and the Good* (Oxford: Oxford University Press, 2010).

13. G. E. Moore, *Principia Ethica* (Cambridge: Cambridge University Press, 1903), p. 27.

14. Agnes Callard, *Aspiration: The Agency of Becoming* (Oxford: Oxford University Press, 2018), p. 72.

15. Talbot Brewer, *The Retrieval of Ethics* (Oxford: Oxford University Press, 2009), p. 37.

16. Klein, "The Penumbral Theory of Masochistic Pleasure."

17. For further elaboration of this example, see my "Finding the Good in Grief: What Augustine Knew That Meursault Could Not."

18. Adam Swenson, "Pain's Evils," *Utilitas* 21 (2009): 197–216.

19. Again, such individuals may not know what the value of that larger activity is. It may be that the pregnant mother desires the pains of childbirth with only an inchoate grasp of what might be valuable about a birthing experience that is painful but "natural."

20. Jollimore, "Meaningless Happiness and Meaningful Suffering."

Chapter 5. Reason in the Midst of Grieving

1. One logical possibility here is that grief is necessarily *rational*. I see no reason in support of such a view, so I set it aside.

2. Stephen Wilkinson, "Is 'Normal Grief' a Mental Disorder?" *Philosophical Quarterly* 50 (2000): 297.

3. See section 4.5.

4. Hyu Jung Huh et al., "Attachment Styles, Grief Responses, and the Moderating Role of Coping Strategies in Parents Bereaved by the Sewol Ferry Accident," *European Journal of Psychotraumatology* 8 (2018). DOI:10.1080/20008198.2018.1424446

5. A similar phenomenon seems in evidence with respect to phobias: Phobics have irrational fears of particular phenomena, but these are not necessarily rooted in irrational or false beliefs about those phenomena (a person who is afraid of spiders need not hold any false beliefs about their dangerousness). "Desensitization" or repeated exposure to the phenomena can effectively treat phobias by retraining "biases" in the phobics' patterns of attention so that the fears do not arise. See J. N. Vrijsen, P. Fleurkens, W. Nieuwboer, and M. Rinck, "Attentional Bias to Moving Spiders in Spider Fearful Individuals," *Journal of Anxiety Disorders* 23 (2009): 541–45.

6. Donald Gustafson, "Grief," *Nous* 23 (1989): 457–79.

7. Gustafson, "Grief," p. 466.

8. Gustafson, "Grief," p. 469.

9. I provide a more thorough critique of Gustafson in my "Grief's Rationality, Backward and Forward," *Philosophy and Phenomenological Research* 94 (2017): 255–72.

10. For a different, albeit somewhat more sympathetic, critical stance on Gustafson's view, Carolyn Price, "The Rationality of Grief," *Inquiry* 53 (2010): 20–40.

11. Such an example also illustrates how evidence of one kind (smell) prompts us to seek out evidence of other kinds (visual, etc.).

12. This is again the phenomenon I've dubbed quasi-grief.

13. Nancy Sherman, "The Moral Logic of Survivor Guilt," *New York Times*, Opinionator, July 3, 2011, https://opinionator.blogs.nytimes.com/2011/07/03/war-and-the-moral-logic-of-survivor-guilt/, accessed March 21, 2020.

14. And of course we have emotions focused on past events (regret, gratitude, etc.).

15. David I. Shalowitz, Elizabeth Garrett-Mayer, and David Wendler, "The Accuracy of Surrogate Decision Makers: A Systematic Review," *Archives of Internal Medicine* 166 (2006): 493–97.

16. Elizabeth K. Vig et al., "Beyond Substituted Judgment: How Surrogates Navigate End-of-Life Decision-Making," *Journal of the American Geriatrics Society* 54 (2006): 1688–93, and Jenna Fritsch et al., "Making Decisions for Hospitalized Older Adults: Ethical Factors Considered by Family Surrogates," *Journal of Clinical Ethics* 24 (2013): 125–34.

17. D. Wendler and A. Rid, "Systematic Review: The Effect on Surrogates of Making Treatment Decisions for Others," *Annals of Internal Medicine* 154 (2011): 336–46.

18. A fuller discussion of this argument can be found in my "Grief and End-of-Life Medical Decision Making," in J. Davis (ed.), *Ethics at the End of Life: New Issues and Arguments* (New York: Routledge, 2017), pp. 201–17.

19. Jessica Mitford, *American Way of Death* (New York: Simon & Schuster, 1963).

20. Caleb Wilde, "Five Ways Funeral Directors Can Bully Their Customers," *Confessions of a Funeral Director*, February 7, 2015, https://www.calebwilde.com/2015/02/five-ways-funeral-directors-can-bully-their-customers/, accessed March 24, 2020.

21. This is not to deny that some grieving individuals make choices that reflect a genuine desire to honor the deceased. Janet McCracken, "Falsely, Sanely, Shallowly: Reflections on the Special Character of Grief," *International Journal of Applied Philosophy* 19 (2005): 147, helpfully calls this the "dedicatory" aspect of grief.

Chapter 6. Our Duty to Grieve

1. Robert Solomon, "On Grief and Gratitude," p. 78.

2. "On Grief and Gratitude," p. 75.

3. "On Grief and Gratitude," p. 81.

4. "On Grief and Gratitude," p. 86.

5. "On Grief and Gratitude," pp. 97–98.

6. "On Grief and Gratitude," p. 98.

7. Though not to say *completely* uncontroversial. Consequentialists about morality are likely to maintain that there is a single fundamental moral duty (to bring about the best possible consequences through our choices and actions), and to the degree that duties are owed to particular individuals, this is merely a contingent fact: that you "owe" a duty to S, a duty to T, etc., is a logical consequence of the fact that fulfilling such duties would bring about the best possible consequences.

8. John Danaher, "The Badness of Grief: A Moderate Defence of the Stoic View," *Philosophical Disquisitions* blog, May 2, 2018, https://philosophicaldisquisitions.blogspot.com.au/2018/05/the-badness-of-grief-moderate-defence.html, accessed May 3, 2018.

9. For an extremely insightful recent investigation of how morally wronging the dead is possible, se David Boonin, *Dead Wrong: The Ethics of Posthumous Harm* (Oxford: Oxford University Press, 2019).

10. Immanuel Kant, *Metaphysics of Morals*, 6:441. For more on Kant's views on duties to oneself, see Jens Timmermann, "Kantian Duties to the Self, Explained and Defended," *Philosophy* 81 (2006): 505–30, and my *Understanding Kant's Ethics* (Cambridge: Cambridge University Press, 2016), pp. 54–60.

11. *Metaphysics of Morals*, 6:419.

12. For more comprehensive defenses of duties to self, see Alison Hills, "Duties and Duties to Self," *American Philosophical Quarterly* 40 (2003): 131–42, and Paul Schofield, *Duty to Self: Moral, Political, and Legal Self-Relation* (Oxford: Oxford University Press, 2021).

13. Stephen Finlay, "Too Much Morality?" in P. Bloomfield (ed.), *Morality and Self-Interest* (Oxford: Oxford University Press, 2008), pp. 140–42.

14. *Justice as Fairness: A Restatement*, E. Kelly (ed.) (Cambridge, MA: Harvard University Press, 2001), pp. 58–60.

15. See, for instance, Thomas E. Hill, Jr., "Servility and Self-Respect," *The Monist* 57 (1973): 87–104, and Carol Hay, *Kantianism, Liberalism, and Feminism: Resisting Oppression* (London: Palgrave Macmillan, 2013).

16. Marcus Singer, "On Duties to Oneself," *Ethics* 69 (1959): 202–5.

17. Tim Oakley, "How to Release Oneself from an Obligation: Good News for Duties to Oneself," *Australasian Journal of Philosophy* 95 (2017): 70–80, and Daniel Muñoz, "The Paradox of Duties to Oneself," *Australasian Journal of Philosophy* 98 (2020): 691–702.

18. The prospect of promises to oneself raise many intricate problems that I set aside here, most notably, how to differentiate a promise to oneself to do X from a mere plan to X or a commitment to X.

19. This line of reasoning echoes that of J. David Velleman, "A Right of Self-Termination?" *Ethics* 109 (1999): 606–28.

Chapter 7. Madness and Medicine

1. Earlier in the play Hamlet complained about Ophelia's emotional capriciousness, particularly the unpredictability of her love.

2. Amy Olberding (personal correspondence) reports that this gender dynamic seems largely absent from discussions of grief in Chinese thought. This is not to say that Asian culture has never depicted grief as a form of feminine madness: Buddhist writings speak of women such as Vasetthi, who, after her son died, wandered the streets naked and lived in trash heaps or graveyards, and Kisagotami, who carried the body of her dead toddler with her as she sought a remedy to restore him to life.

3. M. Stroebe, W. Stroebe, and H. Schut, "Gender Differences in Adjustment to Bereavement: An Empirical and Theoretical Review," *Review of General Psychology* 5 (2001): 62–83. See also Konigsberg, *The Truth about Grief*, chapter 7.

4. Konigsberg, *The Truth About Grief*, especially chapter 6.

5. Dideon, *The Year of Magical Thinking*, p. 34.

6. Wilkinson, "Is 'Normal Grief' a Mental Disorder?" p. 290.

7. A fair-minded overview of this dispute, including the views of those favoring these changes, can be found in Serife Tekin, "Against Hyponarrating Grief: Incompatible Research and Treatment Interests in the DSM-5," in S. Demazeux and P. Singy (eds.), *The DSM-5 in Perspective* (Dordrecht: Springer, 2015), pp. 180–82.

8. Arthur Kleinman, "Culture, Bereavement, and Psychiatry," *The Lancet* 379 (2012): 609.

9. Some insightful discussions of medicalization include Carl Elliott, *Better than Well* (New York: Norton, 2003); Peter Conrad, *The Medicalization of Society*

(Baltimore, MD: Johns Hopkins University Press, 2007); Alison Reiheld, "'Patient complains of . . .': How Medicalization Mediates Power and Justice," *International Journal of Feminist Approaches to Bioethics* 3 (2010): 72–98; and Erik Parens, "On Good and Bad Forms of Medicalization," *Bioethics* 27 (2013): 28–35.

10. James Hawkins, "Complicated Grief—How Common Is It?" *Good Medicine*, January 28, 2016, http://goodmedicine.org.uk/stressedtozest/2015/09/complicated -grief-how-common-it

11. Christopher B. Rosnick, Brent J. Small, and Allison M. Burton, "The Effect of Spousal Bereavement on Cognitive Functioning in a Sample of Older Adults," *Aging, Neuropsychology, and Cognition* 17 (2010): 257–69.

12. H. C. Saavedra Perez, M. A. Ikram, N. Direk, and H. G. Prigerson, "Cognition, Structural Brain Changes and Complicated Grief: A Population-based Study," *Psychological Medicine* 35 (2015): 1389–99.

13. L. Ward, J. L. Mathias, and S. E. Hitchings, "Relationships between Bereavement and Cognitive Functioning in Older Adults," *Gerontology* 53 (2007): 362–72.

14. F. Maccalum and R. A. Bryan, "Attentional Bias in Complicated Grief," *Journal of Affective Disorders* 125 (2010): 316–22.

15. Ward et al., "Relationships between Bereavement and Cognitive Functioning in Older Adults."

16. This is corroborated by studies where test subjects were asked to complete cognitive tasks priming thoughts of death and grief, such as matching or categorizing cards some of which contained words related to death and grief and some of which did not. Maccalum and Bryan, "Attentional Bias in Complicated Grief"; P. J. Freed, T. K. Yanagihara, J. Hirsch, and J. J. Mann, "Neural Mechanisms of Grief Regulation," *Biological Psychiatry* 66 (2009): 33–40; and M. F. O'Connor and B. J. Arizmendi, "Neuropsychological Correlates of Complicated Grief in Older Spousally Bereaved Adults," *Journals of Gerontology B, Psychological Sciences and Social Sciences* 69 (2014): 12–18. N. Schneck et al., "Attentional Bias to Reminders of the Deceased as Compared with a Living Attachment in Grieving," *Biological Psychiatry: Cognitive Neuroscience and Neuroimaging* 3 (2018): 107–15.

17. Mary-Frances O'Connor et al., "Craving Love? Enduring Grief Activates Brain's Reward Center," *NeuroImage* 42 (2008): 969–72.

18. H. Gundel et al., "Functional Neuroanatomy of Grief: An fMRI Study," *American Journal of Psychiatry* 160 (2003): 1946–53; M. F. O'Connor, "Immunological and Neuroimaging Biomarkers of Complicated Grief," *Dialogues in Clinical Neuroscience* 14 (2012): 141–48; A. C. Silva et al., "Neurological Aspects of Grief," *Neurological Disorders* 13 (2014): 930–36.

19. Shulman, *Before and After Loss: A Neurologist's Perspective on Loss, Grief, and Our Brain.*

20. Kay Redfield Jamison, *Nothing Was the Same: A Memoir* (New York: Vintage, 2011), p. 5.

21. Margaret Stroebe, Wolfgang Stroebe, and Georgios Abakoumkin, "The Broken Heart: Suicidal Ideation in Bereavement," *American Journal of Psychiatry* 162 (2005): 2178–80; and N. Molina et al., "Suicidal Ideation in Bereavement: A Systematic Review," *Behavioral Sciences* 9 (2019): 53.

22. Tekin, "Against Hyponarrating Grief," p. 186, expresses the worry by claiming that DSM categories are "hyponarratives" that "bracket the self-related and context-specific aspects" of a "patient's life as whole" to make their disorder no more than a "repertoire" of behaviors. For similar explorations of how mental disorder categories may be therapeutically harmful because they neglect the role of self and self-narration, see Tekin, "Self-concept Through the Diagnostic Looking Glass: Narratives and Mental Disorder," *Philosophical Psychology* 24 (2011): 357–80, and Tekin and Melissa Mosko, "Hyponarrativity and Context-specific Limitations of the DSM-5," *Public Affairs Quarterly* 29 (2015): 109–34.

23. A possibility entertained by Wilkinson, "Is 'Normal Grief' a Mental Disorder?" p. 304.

24. Loretta M. Kopelman, "'Normal Grief' Good or Bad? Health or Disease?'" *Philosophy, Psychiatry, and Psychology* 1 (1995): 209–40.

25. "The Looping Effects of Human Kinds," in D. Sperber, D. Premack, and A. J. Premack (eds.), *Causal Cognition: A Multi-disciplinary Debate* (Oxford: Clarendon Press, 1995), pp. 351–83.

26. Konigsberg, *The Truth About Grief.*

27. See James W. Pennebaker, "Putting Stress into Words: Health, Linguistic, and Therapeutic Implications," *Behavior Research & Therapy* 31(1993): 539–48; and "Writing about Emotional Experiences as a Therapeutic Process," *Psychological Science* 8 (1997): 162–66.

28. On the centrality of storytelling in grief experience, see Paul C. Roseblatt, "Grief across Cultures: A Review and Research Agenda," in W. Stroebe et al. (eds.), *Handbook of Bereavement Research and Practice* (Washington, DC: American Psychological Association, 2008), p. 211.

29. Tekin, "Against Hyponarrating Grief," p. 190.

30. Vaishnav Krishnan and Eric J. Nestler, "The Molecular Neurobiology of Depression," *Nature* 455 (2008): 894–902; and Longfei Yang et al., "The Effects of Psychological Stress on Depression," *Current Neuropharmacology* 13 (2015): 494–504.

Conclusion. Grief Most Human

1. Most zoologists acknowledge that some animal species (whales, primates, elephants, etc.) have some understanding of death and engage in mourning-like death rituals. Disputes arise, however, about whether such animals have the emotional or cognitive repertoire for such behaviors to exemplify grief. See Barbara J. King, *How Animals Grieve* (Chicago: University of Chicago Press, 2008), and Jessica Pierce,

"Do Animals Experience Grief?" *Smithsonian*, August 24, 2018, https://www.smithsonianmag.com/science-nature/do-animals-experience-grief-180970124/

2. Ernest Becker, *The Denial of Death* (New York: Simon & Schuster, 1973); Stephen Cave, *Immorality: The Quest to Live Forever and How It Drives Civilization* (New York: Crown, 2012), pp. 16–21; and Sheldon Solomon, Jeff Greenberg, and Tom Pyszczynski, *The Worm at the Core: The Role of Death in Life* (New York: Random House, 2015).

3. *Breathless*, directed by Jean-Luc Godard (Les Films Impéria, 1960). The line is apparently drawn from William Faulkner's story "The Wild Palms" (New York: Random House, 1939).

4. Julianne Chung, "To Be Creative, Chinese Philosophy Teaches Us to Abandon 'Originality,'" *Psyche*, September 1, 2020, https://psyche.co/ideas/to-be-creative-chinese-philosophy-teaches-us-to-abandon-originality

5. Parallels between the process of grief as I have described it and other traumas are suggested by Susan J. Brison, "Trauma Narratives and the Remaking of the Self," in M. Bal, J. Crewe, and L. Spitzer (eds.), *Acts of Memory: Cultural Recall in the Present* (Hanover, NH: University Press of New England, 1999), pp. 39–54.

6. Chung, "To Be Creative, Chinese Philosophy Teaches Us to Abandon 'Originality.'"

INDEX

DISCUSSION QUESTIONS

1. What are some reasons to consider grief from a philosophical perspective rather than from a psychological or psychiatric perspective?

2. In chapter 1, Michael Cholbi argues that we grieve the deaths of those in whom we have invested our practical identities. What does it mean to have our practical identities invested in someone? How does this explain why people grieve the deaths of those they have never met—for example, political leaders and celebrities?

3. In what ways is grief active? How does it involve attention to a person's relationship to a deceased individual? What is the relationship between grief and mourning?

4. Cholbi writes that "death can produce a relationship crisis for the bereaved." What is this crisis? How does this lead us to think about our own practical identities?

5. What does Cholbi consider the philosophical *paradox of grief*?

6. What good does Cholbi appeal to in order to resolve the paradox of grief? Do you find his resolution of the paradox convincing? Why or why not?

7. What does Cholbi mean when he calls grief *contingently rational*?

8. What are some ways in which grief can distort the rational choices we make regarding the dying or the dead?

9. Cholbi argues in chapter 6 that we have a moral duty to ourselves to grieve. Why does he reach this conclusion? What do you think about the idea that we can let ourselves down if we do not grieve?

10. Why does Cholbi think we should "resist" medicalizing grief? Given his arguments, what is your perspective on the matter?

11. In your estimation, how is the grief we feel at the deaths of others similar or dissimilar to other traumas and losses that we experience?

12. Cholbi says that "grief represents our human nature in full flower." What does grief represent to you?

13. Has your relationship with grief changed throughout your reading of this book? If so, how?